JOURNEY THROUGH SCRIPTURE

Genesis to Jesus

Participant Workbook

SCOTT AND KIMBERLY HAHN
in association with the
St. Paul Center for Biblical Theology

PUBLISHED BY FRANCISCAN MEDIA
Cincinnati, Ohio

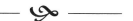

Table of Contents

Student Outlines

Review Notes

Genesis to Jesus
Student Outlines

Lesson One

Studying Scripture From the Heart of the Church

THE BIBLE'S PLOT

Salvation History:

How God's plan of salvation unfolds in the course of human events

Salvation History Time Line

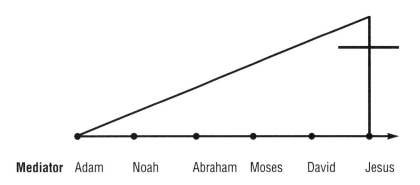

Mediator   Adam   Noah   Abraham   Moses   David   Jesus

LAYING THE FOUNDATION

A Bible study about the Bible

Why should Catholics study the Bible?

How should Catholics study the Bible?

Just a "Protestant thing"?

Theology degree required?

Bad habits?

Catholics read "from the heart of the Church."

EMMAUS ROAD
📖 Luke 24:13-24

The Scriptures show the Christ must suffer.

All of the Scriptures point to Christ.

He teaches them how to read Scripture.

BREAKING THE BREAD
Emmaus (Luke 24:28-30)

Takes bread...

Blesses it…

Breaks it…

Gives it to the disciples

Last Supper (Luke 22:14-20)

Takes bread…

Blesses it…

Breaks it…

Gives it to the disciples

In the Upper Room: The Mass

On the Emmaus Road: The Mass

📖 Luke 24:31–35

Their eyes were opened in the breaking of the bread.

THE MASS IS THE KEY TO THE BIBLE

Scripture → Hearts burn

Breaking of the Bread → Eyes open

Liturgy of the Word and Liturgy of the Eucharist

THE WORD OF GOD

"The Christian faith is not a 'religion of the book.' Christianity is the religion of the 'Word' of God,…'not a written and mute word, but…incarnate and living.' If the Scriptures are not to remain a dead letter, Christ, the eternal Word of the living God, must, through the Holy Spirit, 'open [our] minds to understand the Scriptures'" (CCC 108, quoting St. Bernard, *S. missus est hom. 4*: PL, 183, 86; Luke 24:45).

THE BIBLE AND THE MASS, THEN AND NOW

Revelation 1:3; Colossians 4:16; and 1 Thessalonians 5:27: The believers are to read the apostles' letters in the Church.

Today: Old and New Testament readings

In the Scriptures and the Eucharist, Christ gives us himself.

THE SPIRIT OF TRUTH

📖 John 16:12–14

The Holy Spirit...

Inspires Scripture

Safeguards the Church's interpretation

Guides the Church into all truth

THE DIVINE AUTHOR

📖 2 Timothy 3:16–17

Theopneustos: "God-breathed"

God is "the Principal Author of Scripture" (CCC 304)

The human authors weren't taking down dictation (2 Peter 1:20–21).

THE WORD INCARNATE AND THE WORD INSPIRED

The Word is divine and human.

The Word Incarnate took on all the weaknesses of human flesh…except sin (Hebrews 4:15).

The Word inspired comes to us with all the limitations of human language…except error.

WITHOUT ERROR

"Therefore, since everything asserted by the inspired authors or sacred writers must be held to be asserted by the Holy Spirit, it follows that the books of Scripture must be acknowledged as teaching solidly, faithfully and without error the truth which God wanted put into sacred writings for the sake of our salvation" (*Dei Verbum* 11, www.vatican.va).

THE HUMAN AUTHORS

"The interpreter must investigate what meaning the sacred writer intended to express and actually expressed in particular circumstances by using contemporary literary forms in accordance with the situation of his own time and culture" (*Dei Verbum* 12, www.vatican.va).

THE BIBLE IS LITERATURE

The Bible is a book of books.

Literary "clues" help convey the meaning.

The "literary sense" reveals the plot: God's plan for our salvation.

THE BIBLE IS HISTORICAL

Modern history is secular history: Man's perspective.

Biblical history is sacred history: God's perspective.

It is "His Story."

FROM PROMISE TO FULFILLMENT

Creation in Genesis to a new creation in Revelation (Genesis 1:1; Revelation 21:1)

The cross is at the center.

📖 Galatians 4:4–5

Salvation History: A two-part story

The world before Jesus (promises)

The world after Jesus (fulfillment)

Words are signs.

Chair: what you sit on

God uses history as signs.

⁓

Moses and the Exodus → Christ

Old Testament: Noah, Moses, and David are saviors.

New Testament: Jesus Christ is *the* Savior (Luke 1:68–79, Matthew 28:19–20).

Apostles preach that Jesus is the fulfillment of God's promises (see Acts 13:16–41; 1 Corinthians 10:1–11).

"Thanks to the unity of God's plan, not only the text of Scripture but also the realities and events about which it speaks can be signs" (CCC 117).

Old Testament	New Testament
People	Redeemer
Events	Saving mysteries

THE OLD AND THE NEW

"The New Testament is concealed in the Old and the Old Testament is revealed in the New." St. Augustine

Concealing and revealing = Typology

TYPOLOGY REVEALS GOD'S FATHERLY PLAN

Typology: the study of how Christ was foreshadowed by "types"

The Passover lamb → the Lamb of God (John 1:29; 1 Corinthians 5:7)

Manna → New Manna

📖 John 6:31–35

"Inexhaustible" meanings (CCC 129)

"Dynamic movement" (CCC 130)

We are part of salvation history.

THE BIBLE IS A GIFT FROM GOD

For centuries Christians couldn't afford Bibles.

They heard the Bible at Mass.

The Bible is a family heirloom.

FOR THE SAKE OF OUR SALVATION

2 Timothy 3:16–17: Scripture is inspired by God.

God stoops down to raise us up.

"In the sacred books the Father who is in heaven meets His children with great love and speaks with them" (*Dei Verbum* 21, www.vatican.va).

ALL OF LIFE UNDER THE AUTHORITY OF GOD'S WORD

Memorize the Word and meditate on it.

📖 Psalm 119:9–11

Teach it to children.

📖 Deuteronomy 6:4–7

Practice the moral law and worship (Nehemiah 8, Exodus 20—24).

THE HOLY SPIRIT SAFEGUARDS INTERPRETATION

📖 2 Thessalonians 2:15: "mouth" and "letter"

Misinterpretation is a danger.

📖 Ephesians 4:11–14

The magisterium guards against misinterpretation.

Scripture *and* Tradition (*Dei Verbum* 10)

STUDYING SCRIPTURE FROM THE HEART OF THE CHURCH

Reading Scripture with the same Spirit who inspired it

God is the source of Scripture's unity.

Keep unity in mind.

One plan to unite all things in Christ

St. Irenaeus

"Understanding…consists in showing why there are a number of covenants with mankind, and in teaching what is the character of each of the covenants" (Irenaeus, *Against Heresies*, book 1, chapter 10, no. 3).

SALVATION HISTORY IS COVENANT HISTORY

Testament = Covenant

Covenants ≠ contracts

Covenants make families.

CONTRACTS VS. COVENANTS

Contracts	Covenants
Promise	Oath
Your Name	God's Name

Goods and services   Persons

Temporary   Permanent

COVENANTS MAKE FAMILIES

God makes us his family through covenants.

📖 Jeremiah 31:31–34 (see Ezekiel 36:28)

God is our Father because of his covenant with us (CCC 238).

Salvation history: the story of God becoming *our* Father

WHERE WE ARE NOW

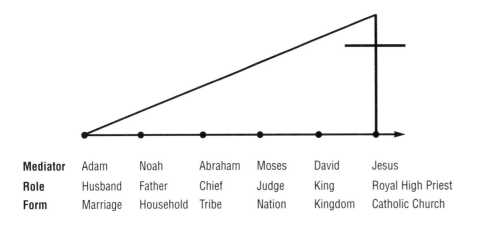

Salvation History Time Line

Mediator	Adam	Noah	Abraham	Moses	David	Jesus
Role	Husband	Father	Chief	Judge	King	Royal High Priest
Form	Marriage	Household	Tribe	Nation	Kingdom	Catholic Church

This study: God's plan and our place in it

Our goal: to become like the disciples on the Emmaus Road

QUESTIONS FOR REVIEW

1. What are the key elements common to the narrative of the road to Emmaus, the Last Supper accounts, and the Catholic celebration of the Mass?

2. What is the relationship between the Holy Spirit and Sacred Scripture?

3. How is biblical history different from secular history? How are they alike?

4. What is typology? How does it unify the Old and New Testaments?

5. What is the difference between a covenant and a contract?

QUESTIONS FOR DISCUSSION

1. Read Psalm 1. What is the attitude of the psalmist toward the Law? Why would the psalmist view the Law with such a grateful heart and want to meditate on it all of the time (see Psalm 19:7–10)?

2. How can we improve our own contemplation of the law of the Lord? What practices could be helpful in this?

3. Read Psalm 119:9–11. What difference could memorizing Scripture make in our daily lives?

4. We know that Scripture teaches "without error." So what do we do when we find a passage of Scripture that seems to contradict what we know about science or seems to contradict another passage?

5. How does the Church teach us to love and to revere Scripture during the Mass?

RECOMMENDED VERSES TO MEMORIZE

Hebrews 4:12

2 Peter 1:20

2 Timothy 3:16–17

Psalm 119:9, 11

FOLLOW-UP READING AND PREPARATION FOR NEXT LESSON

Genesis 1:3 (*The Revised Standard Version* Catholic Edition, available from Ignatius Press or Scepter Press, is recommended)

A Father Who Keeps His Promises: God's Covenant Love in Scripture, by Scott Hahn (Cincinnati: Servant, 1998), chapters 1—3

Dei Verbum, a Vatican II document

Catechism of the Catholic Church (CCC) 112–114, 386–412

For more information on Scripture and Tradition, see Scott Hahn's *Scripture Matters: Essays on Reading the Bible From the Heart of the Church* (Emmaus Road, 2003).

Lesson Two

The Creation Covenant

IN THE BEGINNING

God makes a covenant with creation in Genesis 1:1—2:15

A "covenant with day and night" (Jeremiah 33:25)

God created us to be his family (Genesis 1:26).

CREATION AND EVOLUTION

Creation account: Revealed truth about the *absolute origin* of matter and spirit

Evolution: A scientific theory about the *development* of organisms

Genesis tells us the *what* and *why* of creation, not *how*.

AND GOD SAID...

"Let there be..."

"By the word of the LORD the heavens were made.... For he spoke, and it came to be" (Psalm 33:6-9).

Jesus is the Word by which God created (John 1:1-3; Colossians 1:16-17; Hebrews 1:2).

THE PATTERN OF CREATION

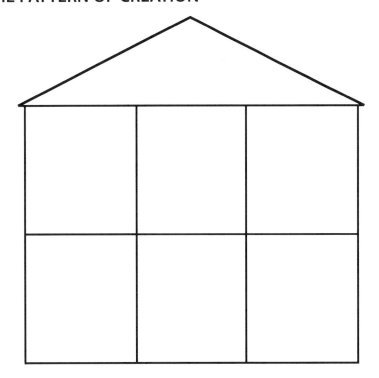

IMAGE AND LIKENESS

Genesis 1:26–27: Man was created in God's "image and likeness."

Genesis 5:1–3: Adam's son Seth was made in his "image and likeness."

"Image and likeness" = sonship

📖 Luke 3:38

WORKING FOR THE WEEKEND

The seventh day finishes God's design.

It was a gift.

All work is ordered to worship.

Creation is the "first and universal witness to God's all powerful love" (CCC 288; see Genesis 15:5; Jeremiah 33:19-26).

SABBATH: SIGN OF GOD'S CREATION COVENANT

Swearing a covenant oath: *sheba* ("to seven oneself")

Abraham offers *seven* lambs (Genesis 21:25–32).

God created the world for a covenant relationship with himself (Jeremiah 33:25–26).

The Sabbath is a perpetual covenant and sign (Exodus 31:16–17).

THE TRUE MEANING OF THE WORLD

The world is a temple.

Job 38:4–11

The foundation

The measurements

The bases

The cornerstone

The bars and doors

God blesses and hallows the Sabbath; Moses blesses the tabernacle (Genesis 2:3; Exodus 39:43; 40:9).

In both instances God declares the Sabbath holy (Genesis 2:2–4; Exodus 31:12–17).

Solomon's temple: seven years, seventh month, seventh day of a seven-day feast, seven petitions (1 Kings 6—8)

Creation and temple: Same language, images, and metaphors

GENESIS 1 AND 2
Genesis 1: God the Creator

Makes a temple

Calls man and woman to imitate him

"Be fruitful and multiply"

"Subdue" creation

Kingly dominion

Genesis 2: God the Father

Fashions the man

Breathes life into him

Creates a garden paradise

Creates his spouse

Priestly guardianship (Genesis 2:15; Numbers 8:24-26; 18:4-5)

ADAM IS THE HIGH PRIEST OF HUMANITY

In ancient times fathers were also priests.

Firstborn sons inherited the priesthood.

Jesus is the firstborn son, king, and eternal high priest (Romans 5:14; Hebrews 1:6; 5:5; 7:15-22; Revelation 1:6; 1 Peter 2:9).

Salvation History Time Line

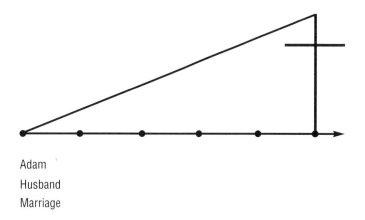

Adam
Husband
Marriage

THE MARRIAGE COVENANT IN GOD'S PLAN

God created man and woman to live in a covenant relationship (CCC 1602).

Marriage: a "sign" of his covenant love

At the beginning in the Garden; at the end in the marriage supper of the Lamb (Revelation 19:9; 21:1–9; 22:17)

JOHN PAUL II

"God in his deepest mystery is not a solitude but a family because he has within himself Fatherhood, Sonship, and the essence of the Family, which is Love" (*Puebla: A Pilgrimage of Faith* [Boston: Daughters of St. Paul, 1979], p. 86).

WE IMAGE THE DIVINE FAMILY

Human families image the Trinity.

The love of the Father and Son becomes a Third Person.

Where two become one, a child comes (Genesis 2:24).

TEMPTATION AND THE FALL: MAKING SENSE OF THE STORY

"The account of the fall in *Genesis* 3 uses figurative language, "but affirms a primeval event, a deed that took place *at the beginning of the history of man*. "Revelation gives us the certainty of faith that the whole of human history is marked by the original fault freely committed by our first parents." (CCC 390; see *Gaudium et Spes* 13 §1; Council of Trent: DS 1513; Pius XII: DS 3897; Paul VI: AAS 58 [1966])

GOD PREPARES ADAM FOR THE TEST
📖 Genesis 2:15–17

Adam is to guard the garden.

God places a limitation on Adam.

God gives Adam a warning.

God gives Adam Eve, his helpmate (Genesis 2:18–24).

ADAM AND EVE ARE READY
God breathed into Adam "the breath of life."

Adam was in a state of grace (CCC 375).

Adam and Eve were more than capable.

THE THREAT OF THE SERPENT

Serpent: *Nahash* [nuh hawsh?]

Numbers 21:6–9: "fiery serpents"

Isaiah 27:1–3: "Leviathan, the fleeing serpent," "the twisting serpent," the "dragon that is in the sea"

Revelation 12:3, 9: the "great, red dragon," the "ancient serpent who is called the Devil and Satan," and the "deceiver" of the world

THE TEST OF THEIR LIVES

📖 Genesis 3:1–6

Four questions

As son, will Adam trust?

As king, will Adam guard?

As husband, will Adam protect?

As priest, will Adam sacrifice?

DID ADAM AND EVE DIE?

Adam and Eve lose divine life.

Mortal sin leads to spiritual death (CCC 403).

Later they die physically.

PRIDE AND DISOBEDIENCE: FAILING THE TEST OF LOVE

Adam failed to guard.

Adam failed to speak.

Adam failed to lead.

Adam failed to sacrifice (CCC 397–398).

GOD CONFRONTS ADAM AND EVE

Genesis 3:8: the "sound [*qol*] of the Lord God"

Psalm 29:1–9

"powerful"

"full of majesty"

"breaks the cedars of Lebanon"

"flashes forth with flames of fire"

"shakes the wilderness"

"makes the oaks to whirl and strips the forest bare"

📖 Genesis 3:9–13

COVENANT CURSES

The Serpent: humiliation and destruction (Genesis 3:14)

Enmity between the Serpent's seed and the woman's (Genesis 3:15–19)

Childbirth will be painful.

Relationships marred by sin

Work will be toil—thorns and thistles.

Physical death

THE FIRST GOSPEL

The seed of the woman will triumph (Genesis 3:15).

This promise is the *Protoevangelium*.

The "seed of the woman" implies the Virgin Birth.

JESUS IS THE NEW ADAM

This New Adam will achieve victory.

The New Eve will be his mother.

📖 Romans 5:17–19

Death through the first Adam and Eve; life through the New Adam and New Eve (1 Corinthians 15:21–22, 45–49)

THE POWER OF FEAR AND DEATH DESTROYED

📖 Hebrews 2:14–15

Jesus goes into a garden (Matthew 26:36–46).

Sweats drops of blood (Luke 22:44)

A crown of thorns (Matthew 27:29)

Stripped naked (Matthew 27:28, 31, 35)

Goes to the Tree of Life (Acts 5:30)

SELF-OFFERING

Christ gives the perfect example of self-offering.

Through that offering he restores what Adam lost (2 Peter 1:4).

Mary does the opposite of Eve (Luke 1:38).

GOD'S ABUNDANT MERCY

God makes merciful provisions for humanity and Adam and Eve.

Covers their nakedness (Genesis 3:21)

Banishes them from Eden

UNDERSTANDING THE TEST

The Bible is the story of God's love for his people.

Covenant love requires total self-giving.

In the Bible God raises his family from infancy to adulthood.

REVIEW QUESTIONS FOR PERSONAL STUDY

How is God's creation like the tabernacle and the temple?

How is Adam both a royal firstborn son and a priest?

Where do we find the first promise of a savior who will redeem the human race?

—— ❧ ——

Read Romans 5:12–21. How does St. Paul contrast the old Adam with the New Adam, Christ? What sign did God give us at creation that reveals who he is?

QUESTIONS FOR DISCUSSION

1. Look at Genesis 1:26–28. What does it mean to say that God created man and woman "in his own image"? How do we "image" God?

2. What were Adam's missteps? his failures? Does this tell us anything about men's struggles to grow in holiness and live as sons of God? If so, what?

3. What were Eve's missteps? her failures? Does this tell us anything about women's struggles to grow in holiness and live as daughters of God? If so, what?

4. Does the Serpent tempt us in ways similar to how he tempted Adam and Eve? If so, how?

5. How do we see the effects of Adam and Eve's punishment (the curses) at work in men, women, and the world today?

RECOMMENDED VERSES TO MEMORIZE

Genesis 1:1–2

Genesis 1:26

Genesis 3:15

FOLLOW-UP READING AND PREPARATION FOR LESSON 3

Genesis 4—11

A Father Who Keeps His Promises, chapters 3 and 4

Lesson Three

Noah and a Renewed Creation

INTRODUCTION

"Even when [man] disobeyed you and lost your friendship you did not abandon him to the power of death.... Again and again you offered a covenant to man" (CCC 55, quoting *Roman Missal*, Eucharistic Prayer IV, 118).

Christ comes "in the fullness of time" (Galatians 4:4).

THE TWO SEEDS

Adam and Eve's first two sons, Cain and Abel

"By faith Abel offered to God a more acceptable sacrifice" (Hebrews 11:4).

Cain's "deeds were evil" (1 John 3:12).

Cain defies God and kills his brother (Genesis 4:8).

GOD CONFRONTS CAIN

God questions Cain (Genesis 4:9–10).

Cain refuses to confess (Genesis 4:13–14).

The ground will not yield fruit, and he is cast out (Genesis 4:11–12).

Covenant curses: an extreme form of fatherly punishment

ADAM'S FAMILY DIVIDED

Cain
Builds a city named [*shem*]
after his son (Genesis 4:17).
Seventh generation: Lamech,
bigamist and murderer

Seth
"Call upon the name [*shem*] of the
Lord" (Genesis 4:26).
Seventh generation: Enoch "walked with
God" (Genesis 5:24; see Hebrews 11:5).

MIXED MARRIAGES

"They took to wife such of them as they chose" (Genesis 6:2).

Their sons embraced wickedness.

"Men of renown" = "Men of the name [*shem*]" (Genesis 6:4)

SAVED THROUGH WATER

"All flesh had corrupted their way.... The earth [was] filled with violence" (Genesis 6:12–13, see also 6:5).

Only Noah "walked with God" (Genesis 6:9).

Noah and his family will be the righteous remnant.

God instructs Noah to build an ark.

By faith "Noah…did all that God commanded him" (Genesis 6:22; see Hebrews 11:7).

A witness to judgment *and* mercy

A NEW CREATION
📖 Genesis 6:18

First use of *covenant* (*berith*)

Establish (*heqim*) implies renewal.

A new world emerges from the deep (Genesis 1:2; 7:11).

The Flood begins after seven days (Genesis 2:2; 7:10).

The ark rests on dry land in the seventh month (Genesis 2:2–3; 8:4).

Noah sends out a bird every seven days (Genesis 8:10–12).

Seven pairs of every clean animal on the ark (Genesis 7:2)

Rainbow: Sign of God's renewed covenant

The covenant is renewed through sacrifice.

📖 Genesis 8:20–22

Salvation History Time Line

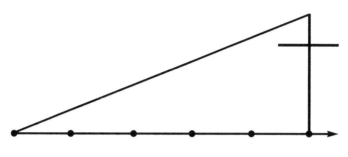

Mediator	Adam	Noah
Role	Husband	Father
Form	Marriage	Household

A NEW ADAM

"Be fruitful and multiply" (Genesis 1:28; 9:1).

"…have dominion" (Genesis 1:28; 9:2).

A garden to inhabit (Genesis 2:15; 9:20)

Fruit that exposes nakedness (Genesis 3:6–7; 9:21)

THE TABLE OF NATIONS

Noah's seventy descendants and the nations of the world (Genesis 10)

Reveals God's fatherly perspective

Shows original unity and pattern of sin and judgment

The people of God are the bearers of God's blessing.

ONE BIG BROKEN FAMILY (AGAIN)
Through Shem's descendants God continues to build his covenant family.

Israel descends from Shem (Shemites or Semites).

Shem was the great-grandfather of Eber (Hebrews).

Eber → the Hebrews → Israelites → Jesus of Nazareth

Ham → Ancient Israel's enemies

The Egyptians

The Canaanites

The Philistines

The Assyrians

The Babylonians

THE TOWER OF BABEL

Ham's descendants seek to establish their name, their *shem* (Genesis 11:4).

Shem's descendants seek to advance the Lord's name.

Babel: the "perversion of paganism" (CCC 57)

Judgment: confused and scattered

THE COVENANT WITH NOAH

God's covenant with Noah was far-reaching.

God still cares for the nations.

"The covenant with Noah remains in force during the times of the Gentiles, until the universal proclamation of the Gospel" (CCC 58).

A FLOOD OF COMPARISONS

The covenant with Noah points to baptism.

📖 1 Peter 3:20–21

The Flood is a type of baptism (CCC 701, 1219).

Baptism destroys sin.

"New creations"

A warning

Ham squandered his salvation.

Baptism alone can't assure us of salvation.

We have to cooperate with God's plan.

LITERARY FRAMEWORK OF GENESIS 1—11

Literary framework reveals:

Salvation history is shaped by spiritual conflict.

Righteousness and wickedness travel through family lines.

God vindicates and judges.

Narrative Structure

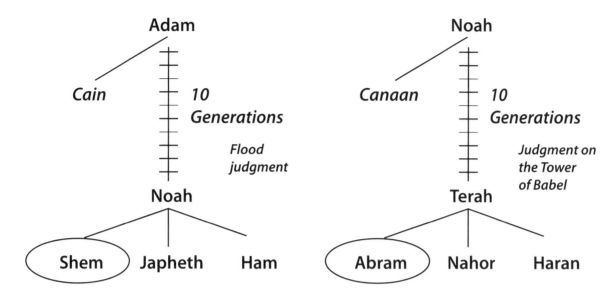

"Generations" (*toledoth*) connect stories.

"These are the generations [*toledoth*] of the heavens and the earth" (Genesis 2:4).

"This is the book of the generations of Adam" (Genesis 5:1).

"These are the generations of Noah" (Genesis 6:9).

Generations (*toledoth*) appears ten times.

Reveals deliberative literary framework

God's perspective is family.

Conflict between

The two seeds (Genesis 3:15)

The two sons (Genesis 4—5)

The two lines

St. Augustine

The City of God

The City of Man

QUESTIONS FOR REVIEW

1. What is the primary, underlying sin of both Cain's and Ham's descendants?

2. How is the story of Noah and the Flood like the Creation account?

3. How does the Flood prefigure baptism?

4. How does Christ fulfill the Creation covenant?

QUESTIONS FOR DISCUSSION

1. Is God's punishment of Cain merciful? Why or why not?

2. What does the story of Noah and the Flood teach us about justice? about mercy?

3. What can we learn from Noah about the virtue of obedience?

4. In what ways are the sins of our culture like the sins of Cain's and Ham's descendants?

5. How can we raise a godly family as Noah did in the midst of an often hostile culture?

RECOMMENDED VERSES TO MEMORIZE

Hebrews 11:1

1 Peter 3:21

FOLLOW-UP READING AND PREPARATION FOR THE NEXT LESSON

Genesis 12; 15; 17; 22

A Father Who Keep His Promises, chapter 5

Lesson Four

Abraham: Our Father in Faith

AND GOD BLESSED THEM

Life reveals blessing.

That blessing is passed on through families.

God's covenant blessing is restored through Noah and passed on through Shem (Genesis 9:1, 26).

FATHERLY BLESSING

God promises to bless Abraham and all humanity through him (Genesis 12:1–3).

This blessing will be transmitted through Abraham's descendants.

True unity will come through God making Abraham's name (*shem*) great.

Salvation History Time Line

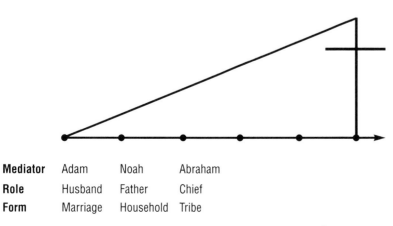

Mediator	Adam	Noah	Abraham
Role	Husband	Father	Chief
Form	Marriage	Household	Tribe

THE THREE PROMISES OF GENESIS 12
📖 Genesis 12:1–3

1. Land and nationhood

2. A royal dynasty (a "great name"; see 2 Samuel 7:9)

3. A worldwide family

Three Promises → three covenant oaths

ABRAM RESPONDS IN FAITH
Abram is seventy-five years old, wealthy, and childless.

He leaves to begin a nomadic life of wandering (Genesis 12:4–9).

He did all this in faith (Hebrews11:8).

THE TESTS OF THE BLESSED
Famine (Genesis 12)

Exile and the temporary loss of his wife (Genesis 12)

Family strife and division (Genesis 13)

Wars (Genesis 14)

Unfulfilled promises (Genesis 15)

Marital discord (Genesis 16)

Painful surgery (Genesis 17)

Supernatural disaster (Genesis 18—19)

The temporary loss of his wife, again (Genesis 20)

More family strife (Genesis 21)

Asked to sacrifice his son (Genesis 22)

His faith is rewarded (Genesis 15; 17; 22)

📖 Hebrews 6:13-17

GOD BLESSES ABRAM THROUGH MELCHIZEDEK
Priest-king of Salem ("peace") (Genesis 14:17-20)

Offers bread and wine, blesses Abram, receives homage

Christ, a Priest-King, offers bread and wine, receives homage.

📖 Hebrews 6:19—7:2

THE FIRST COVENANT OATH
A son and innumerable descendants

Delivery from bondage and the Promised Land

God seals the covenant with sacrifice (Genesis 15:7–21).

ABRAM'S OTHER SON
Sarai offers Hagar (Genesis 16:1–3).

Hagar conceives and looks upon Sarai "with contempt" (Genesis 16:4).

Ishmael becomes the father of the Arabs.

THE SECOND COVENANT OATH
Abram →Abraham, "father of a multitude" (Genesis 17:5)

Sarai →Sarah, "great mother" (Genesis 17:15)

From Sarah "kings of peoples shall come" (Genesis 17:16).

Sarah will give birth to a son in one year (Genesis 17:21).

Circumcision comes first (Genesis 17:9–14).

Circumcision for all on the eighth day

Abraham's obedience reveals his tremendous faith.

ISAAC AND ISHMAEL

Sarah gives birth to Isaac.

Abraham throws a great feast (Genesis 21:8).

Sarah asks Abraham to banish Ishmael (Genesis 21:10).

God promises to make a great nation out of Ishmael's descendants.

THE FINAL COVENANT OATH

God asks Abraham to sacrifice Isaac on Mount Moriah.

Abraham doesn't hesitate.

Isaac carries the wood for the sacrifice up the hill (Genesis 22:6).

"Where is the lamb for the…offering?" (Genesis 22:7).

"God will provide himself the lamb" (Genesis 22:8).

SOWING SEEDS OF FUTURE BLESSING

Genesis 22:18 echoes Genesis 3:15.

Deliverance through the "seed" of the woman

Deliverance through the "seed" of Abraham

Both seeds refer to Christ.

📖 Galatians 3:14–17

THE OBEDIENCE OF ABRAHAM AND ISAAC

When Adam disobeyed, humanity was cursed.

When Abraham obeyed, humanity was blessed.

Through Abraham's seed the curses of the Fall will be reversed.

Aqedah: "the binding of Isaac"

Isaac's self-offering

Isaac could have resisted.

Jewish tradition: Isaac was bound at his own request.

ONLY BELOVED SON OF THE FATHER

Jesus is the only beloved Son of the Father (Genesis 22:2; Matthew 3:17; John 3:16)

Jesus carried the wood of his sacrifice (Genesis 22:6; Luke 23:26).

Both fathers receive their sons back on the third day (Hebrews 11:19; Genesis 22:4; 1 Corinthians 15:4).

MY BELOVED SON

On Mount Tabor: "This is my beloved Son" (Mark 9:7).

"Take your son, your only…son Isaac, whom you love…" (Genesis 22:2).

God did not stop the death of his beloved Son.

"GOD WILL PROVIDE HIMSELF THE LAMB"

The Lord provided himself as the Lamb.

Moriah: part of a chain of mountains outside Jerusalem

The temple of Jerusalem was built on Moriah (2 Chronicles 3:1).

Calvary is one of the peaks of Moriah.

THREE PROMISES STRENGTHENED BY OATHS

Three promises to Abraham:

Land → Genesis 15 → Mosaic covenant

Kingship →Genesis 17 → Davidic covenant

Worldwide blessing → Genesis 22 → new covenant

THE ELDER SHALL SERVE THE YOUNGER

Isaac's two sons: Jacob and Esau

Jacob is chosen over Esau.

Joseph will be chosen over his older brothers.

This subplot runs throughout the Bible.

Older sons fall like Adam.

God's plans are fulfilled through his power.

"In order that God's purpose of election might continue, not because of works but because of his call,…so it depends not on man's will or exertion but upon God's mercy" (Romans 9:11, 16).

THE REST OF THE STORY

God changes Jacob's name to Israel.

Israel has twelve sons.

The twelve sons journey into Egypt.

Israel gives Joseph a beautiful coat.

Jealous older brothers sell him into slavery.

God blesses Joseph with the gift of interpreting dreams.

Joseph becomes prime minister.

Joseph's brothers come to Egypt for food.

The family is reunited.

The family stays in Egypt.

A new Pharaoh arises.

He enslaves the sons of Israel.

"God will be with you, and will bring you again to the land of your fathers" (Genesis 48:21).

Genesis 15: Abraham's descendants will be delivered from slavery.

QUESTIONS FOR REVIEW

1. What are the three promises God makes to Abraham in Genesis 12:1–3?

2. How do the three promises relate to the covenant oaths God swears in Genesis 15, 17, and 22?

3. What is the relationship of these covenant promises to future events in salvation history?

4. How does Abraham's offering of his beloved son Isaac help us understand God the Father's offering of Jesus for the atonement for our sins?

5. How does the phrase "the elder shall serve the younger" describe a subplot of Scripture? What lesson should we draw from this subplot?

QUESTIONS FOR DISCUSSION

1. What can we learn from Abraham's obedience to God's call? How must that obedience have looked to his peers? Discuss how God's call to Christians today might elicit similar reactions from the culture.

2. Discuss Abraham's example of faith. What trials did he face? What does this tell us about the relationship between blessings and trials?

3. What does the story of Abraham's offering of Isaac teach us about God's fatherly sacrifice for us?

4. What does Isaac's self-offering teach us about Jesus' self-offering?

5. What can we learn from Abraham's example of total surrender?

RECOMMENDED VERSES TO MEMORIZE
Genesis 12:1–3

John 3:16

FOLLOW-UP READING AND PREPARATION FOR NEXT LESSON
Exodus 1—3; 4:21–23; 12; 19; 24:1; 25:9; 32

Ezekiel 20:1–26

A Father Who Keeps His Promises, chapters 7—9

Lesson Five

Moses and the Israelites

THE STORY OF GOD'S FIRSTBORN SON

Salvation history is the story of God's family.

Adam was the firstborn son of creation.

Adam falls, but God remains faithful.

Humanity will be restored through Abraham.

God's covenant family becomes a nation.

Israel is God's "firstborn."

Like Adam, Israel fails.

God stoops down to raise the Israelites up.

ABRAHAM'S FAMILY LINE

Abraham was the father of Isaac.

Isaac was the father of Jacob (Israel) (Genesis 35:9–13).

Israel had twelve sons.

Twelve sons became the fathers of the twelve tribes.

Twelve tribes became slaves in Egypt.

Salvation History Time Line

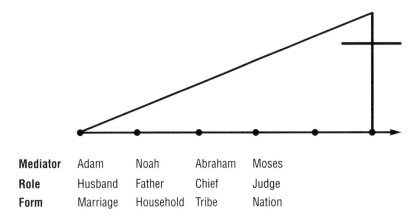

Mediator	Adam	Noah	Abraham	Moses
Role	Husband	Father	Chief	Judge
Form	Marriage	Household	Tribe	Nation

LIBERTY OR DEATH

Abraham's descendants will be enslaved, but God will deliver them (Genesis 15:13-14).

Pharaoh enslaves the Hebrews (Exodus 1:8-14).

Israel cries out to God for help.

📖 Exodus 2:23-25

MOSES' EARLY LIFE

Pharaoh orders the death of all newborn Hebrew males (Exodus 1:15-22).

Jochebed defies Pharaoh (Exodus 2:1-4).

Pharaoh's daughter finds Moses (Exodus 2:5-9).

Moses is raised by Pharaoh's daughter (Exodus 2:10).

📖 Exodus 2:11–16

Moses settles in Midian.

THE CALL OF MOSES
📖 Exodus 3:1–8

God tells Moses his plan.

Request a three-day journey into the wilderness for worship.

God will judge Egypt and lead Israel into the Promised Land.

The Lord will take Pharaoh's firstborn son (Exodus 4:22–23).

THE GODS OF EGYPT
Israel must sacrifice cattle, sheep, and goats.

Those sacrifices would be an abomination to the Egyptians (Exodus 8:25–27).

Israel was to sacrifice objects of idolatry.

MORE THAN POLITICAL LIBERATION

God wanted to lead Israel out of spiritual bondage.

📖 Ezekiel 20:6–9

"Let my people go, that they may serve me in the wilderness" (Exodus 7:16).

"Serve" = "ministry"

THE PLAGUES OF EGYPT

Numbers 33:3–4: The plagues symbolize judgment on Egypt's gods.

Nile into blood → victory over Nile god Hapi (Exodus 7:14–25)

Frogs → mocks the frog goddess Hecket (Exodus 8:1)

Cattle killed → judgment on the bull gods Apis and Hathor (Exodus 9:1–7)

Plague of darkness → defeat of the sun god Ra (Exodus 10:21–29)

THE TENTH PLAGUE

Exodus 11:1, 4–9; 12:28–36: The angel of death will slay the firstborns.

Exodus 9:4; 12:1–14: To be spared, Israelites must

sacrifice an unblemished lamb,

spread its blood over their doorposts,

and eat it as part of a sacred meal.

BAPTIZED INTO MOSES

Soon after deliverance the complaining starts.

They're thirsty (Exodus 15:22–25).

They're hungry (Exodus 16:1–4, 35).

They're thirsty again (Exodus 17:1–7).

📖 1 Corinthians 10:1–6 Foreshadowing the new covenant

Baptism

Eucharist

THE FIRST COVENANT WITH ISRAEL

The Israelites arrive at Mount Sinai.

God will make them a "holy nation," a "royal priesthood" (Exodus 19:5–6).

The Ten Commandments will help them obey (Exodus 20:1-17; 32:15-16).

So will the Book of the Covenant (civil laws) (Exodus 21—23).

📖 Exodus 24:3-8: "The blood of the covenant"

📖 Exodus 24:9-11: A covenantal meal

THE TABERNACLE

God gives Moses a vision of the tent of worship (Exodus 25:9).

The earthly tent and temple were to be copies of heavenly counterparts.

📖 Hebrews 8:5

Isaiah sees the original.

📖 Isaiah 6:1-3

John describes the heavenly temple in Revelation 21; 22.

God's purpose is to

Teach Israel to live holy lives

Bring Israel into his presence through worship

Dwell in communion with him as family

THE GOLDEN CALF

In despair the Israelites revert to idolatry (Exodus 32:1-6).

They succumb to the three ancient temptations:

Money

Sex (Exodus 32:6)

Power

GOD "REMEMBERS" HIS OATH

📖 Exodus 32:7-10

No longer "my people"

Moses reminds God of his covenant with Abraham (Exodus 32:13-14).

God "programmed" the covenant with mercy.

ISRAEL BREAKS THE COVENANT

Moses smashes the Ten Commandments (Exodus 32:15–19).

"Who is on the LORD's side?" (Exodus 32:26).

Only the Levites (Exodus 32:26)

Three thousand die by the Levites' swords (Exodus 32:27–29).

"Today you have ordained yourselves for the service of the LORD" (Exodus 32:29).

GOD'S SECOND COVENANT WITH ISRAEL

The Israelites are still in spiritual bondage.

God gives them ritual purity laws.

These quarantine Israel.

Israel is not ready to evangelize the nations.

Animal sacrifice is now required.

They must regularly renounce the gods of Egypt through sacrifice.

THE LEVITICAL PRIESTS

God's original call: A kingdom of priests (Exodus 19:6)

Now only the Levites will serve as priests (Numbers 1–6).

The Book of Leviticus

Explains the purity laws (Leviticus 1—16)

And the laws the Levites are to teach to the people (Leviticus 17—26)

THE BOOK OF NUMBERS

Numbers: More sin → more laws

St. Paul: Laws were given to teach Israel their weakness and get them to turn to the Lord.

📖 Galatians 3:19

The Israelites come to the borders of the Promised Land.

Numbers 13:30—14:10: The Israelites panic.

Only Joshua and Caleb trust God will help them reconquer the land.

Of this generation only Joshua and Caleb will eventually enter.

DEUTERONOMY

Idolatry at Ba'al Peor → another set of laws

"Deuteronomy": "Second law"

Promulgated in the words of Moses

Concessions include divorce and genocidal warfare.

📖 Matthew 19:8

Concessions exist because of the hardness of their hearts.

"I gave them statutes that were not good and ordinances by which they could not have life" (Ezekiel 20:25).

Deuteronomy: How God fathers men

Galatians 3:24: The Law is like a child's tutor.

The Deuteronomic law tried to teach Israel how to "grow up."

The laws bound Israel until the coming of Christ.

PLANS FOR THE SANCTUARY

Detailed instructions for reconquest

Once Israel has "rest from all [their] enemies," they will build God a temple (Deuteronomy 12:10-11).

Relationship with God and worship are the real goals.

JESUS AS THE NEW MOSES

Born during the reign of a ruthless king

All other Hebrew male children killed

Escapes slaughter and finds safety in Egypt

Called back to birthplace after a time in exile

Passes through water and tested in the wilderness

Fasts forty days and forty nights

Turns water into wine, then wine into blood

Teaches from a mountain (the Sermon on the Mount)

Transfigured, radiating God's glory

Gives heavenly bread and spiritual drink—the New Manna

Appoints twelve leaders, then seventy

The true Passover Lamb

Leads us out of spiritual bondage in a New Exodus

THE NEW PASSOVER

In Israel's Passover

A lamb was sacrificed.

Its blood was shed.

It was eaten as part of a family meal.

Those who partook were spared from death.

In the New Passover

Christ is the sacrificial Lamb of God.

His blood is shed for the world's salvation.

We must feed upon Christ's Body and Blood.

Through the Eucharist we receive life.

Israel's Passover: God delivers them from slavery and leads them to the Promised Land

New Passover: Christ delivers us from sin and leads us to the true Promised Land

📖 1 Corinthians 5:6–8

📖 Matthew 26:26–28

We eat in God's presence.

QUESTIONS FOR REVIEW

1. In what way does the Book of Exodus show us God's judgment on the gods of the Egyptians?

2. Why did God first instruct Israel to offer animal sacrifices? Why does he later call for regular animal sacrifices?

3. What was the goal of the Exodus?

4. How does Moses prefigure the person and work of Christ?

5. How is the Eucharist the New Passover?

QUESTIONS FOR DISCUSSION

1. Read Exodus 3:13—4:17. What excuses do we make for not following God's lead in our lives?

2. What is the difference between contentment and contentiousness? Read Proverbs 21:9, 19.

3. What can we learn from the Israelites' response to Moses about how we are to respond to the authorities God has placed in our lives, such as our bishops and the pope?

4. How did the people of Israel demonstrate their lack of trust in the Lord? How do we do the same? What can we do to counter that lack of trust?

5. How does God accommodate us and our failings, as he accommodated the Israelites and their failings?

RECOMMENDED VERSES TO MEMORIZE

1 Corinthians 5:7–8

John 1:29

FOLLOW-UP READING AND PREPARATION FOR THE NEXT LESSON

2 Samuel 6—7

Isaiah 9; 53

Jeremiah 31

A Father Who Keeps His Promises, chapter 11

Lesson Six

The Covenant With David

JOSHUA AND THE PROMISED LAND—ENTRANCE AND CONQUEST

The second generation of Israelites enters the Promised Land (Joshua 3:4).

God gives them victory over the inhabitants.

JUDGES: THE CONQUEST CONTINUES

Judges lead the Israelites.

The Cycle of the Three "Ds"

Disobedience

Defeat

Deliverance

1 AND 2 SAMUEL—THE CONQUEST COMPLETED

The Israelites demand that God give them a king.

📖 1 Samuel 8:1–9

Saul is selected.

SAUL, FIRST KING OF ISRAEL

Samuel anoints Saul (1 Samuel 10:1).

Benjamin: The smallest and youngest of the twelve tribes

Success comes from God.

KING SAUL FALLS

Saul's disobedience: 1 Samuel 13:8–11, 13–14

Samuel must offer sacrifices before the battle.

Saul offers sacrifices not his to make.

Saul's pride costs him his dynasty.

Saul disobeys again: 1 Samuel 15:1–3, 8-9.

Saul is to kill *all* the Amalekites and their livestock.

He doesn't.

Saul will now lose his throne (1 Samuel 15:20–23).

God instructs Samuel to anoint David as the new king (1 Samuel 16:11–13).

DAVID RISES TO POWER

With only a slingshot and five stones, David defeats Goliath (1 Samuel 17:38–54).

Saul invites David to live with the royal family.

David becomes close friends with Jonathan, Saul's would-be heir.

Saul plots to kill David (1 Samuel 23:15).

David refuses to harm Saul (1 Samuel 24).

David mourns Saul's and his sons' deaths (2 Samuel 1:19–24).

DAVID WANTS TO BUILD GOD A HOUSE

📖 Deuteronomy 12:10–11: God's ultimate goal for Israel

The conquest of Jerusalem fulfills the conditions of the Deuteronomic covenant.

David wants to build God a temple (2 Samuel 7:1–2).

GOD WILL BUILD A HOUSE FOR DAVID

📖 2 Samuel 7:8–16

God will build David a "house."

Family: God will give David a son (2 Samuel 7:12).

Dynasty: David's royal heir will reign forever (2 Samuel 7:13).

Temple: David's son will build the house of the Lord (2 Samuel 7:13).

Salvation History Time Line

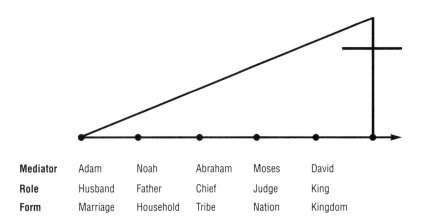

Mediator	Adam	Noah	Abraham	Moses	David
Role	Husband	Father	Chief	Judge	King
Form	Marriage	Household	Tribe	Nation	Kingdom

A KINGDOM OF PRIESTS

Through the Davidic kingdom God extends his covenant to the nations.

God's original plan for Israel: a kingdom of priests who would evangelize nations (Exodus 19:6)

God establishes David as a priest-king.

📖 2 Samuel 6:14, 17–19

David wears a Levitical garment.

He brings the ark of the covenant into Jerusalem.

He offers sacrifices.

He blesses the people.

He feeds them bread, a cake of raisins, and wine.

DAVID AS LITURGICAL LEADER

God gives David the blueprints for the temple (1 Chronicles 28:19).

David organizes the duties of the Levites (1 Chronicles 15—16; 23—26).

He leads the procession of the ark.

He makes thank offerings (Psalms 22; 69; 100; 116).

JESUS AS THE NEW DAVID

2 Samuel 7:8-17	Luke 1:32-33
"A great name"	"He will be great."
"He shall be my son."	"Son of the Most High"
"Establish the throne"	"God…will give him the throne of his father David."
"Forever"	"Reign for ever"

SEVEN PRIMARY FEATURES OF THE DAVIDIC COVENANT
First: The Son of David Is the Son of God
📖 Psalm 89:26–27 (See also 2 Samuel 7:14)

Christ: The eternal firstborn (Hebrews 1:6)

Second: The Davidic King is a Messiah
Messiah (*mashiach*) = "anointed one"

📖 Psalm 89:19–21 Anointing the king symbolized the reception of God's spirit (see also 1 Samuel 16:13; 1 Kings 1:32–40; 2 Kings 11:12, 2; 2 Chronicles 23:11).

In Greek "anointed one" = "Christ"

Jesus is the true anointed one of God (Mark 1:9–11; Luke 1:5; John 1:32).

Third: The Davidic Kingdom is International
David's cabinet includes non-Israelites (1 Chronicles 11:11–12).

Solomon's reign is "to the ends of the earth" (Psalm 72:8–11; 2:8).

Matthew 28:19: Make disciples of "all nations."

Fourth: The Davidic Kingdom in Jerusalem

Jerusalem will be the political and spiritual center.

On Mount Zion all nations will gather before God's presence.

📖 Psalm 87:5

The Upper Room was on Mount Zion.

Christ reigns in the New Jerusalem (Revelation 22:1–5).

Fifth: The Temple of Solomon

1 Kings 8:27–29: The place where God's name dwells

Signifies a new era for Israel

The tabernacle and temple were forerunners.

📖 Hebrews 8:5

The new temple is Christ's body.

📖 John 2:19–22

Sixth: The Wisdom of Solomon

Solomon asks God for wisdom (1 Kings 3).

Solomon's wisdom literature: Proverbs, Ecclesiastes, the Song of Solomon, the Wisdom of Solomon

Christ is "our wisdom" (1 Corinthians 1:30; John 14:26).

Seventh: An Everlasting Kingdom

The longest lasting dynasty in recorded history: four hundred years (2 Samuel 7:13; Psalm 89:36–37)

The Davidic king and his sons are killed in 586 BC (2 Kings 25).

In Christ God honors his oath.

SECONDARY FEATURES OF THE DAVIDIC COVENANT

The *gebirah*, or the queen mother (1 Kings 2:19)

The prime minister (Isaiah 22:15–25)

The *todah*, or thank offering (see Leviticus 7:11–21; 1 Chronicles 16)

THE PSALMS AND THE THANK OFFERING

📖 Psalm 50:14–15

"Offer to God a sacrifice of thanksgiving

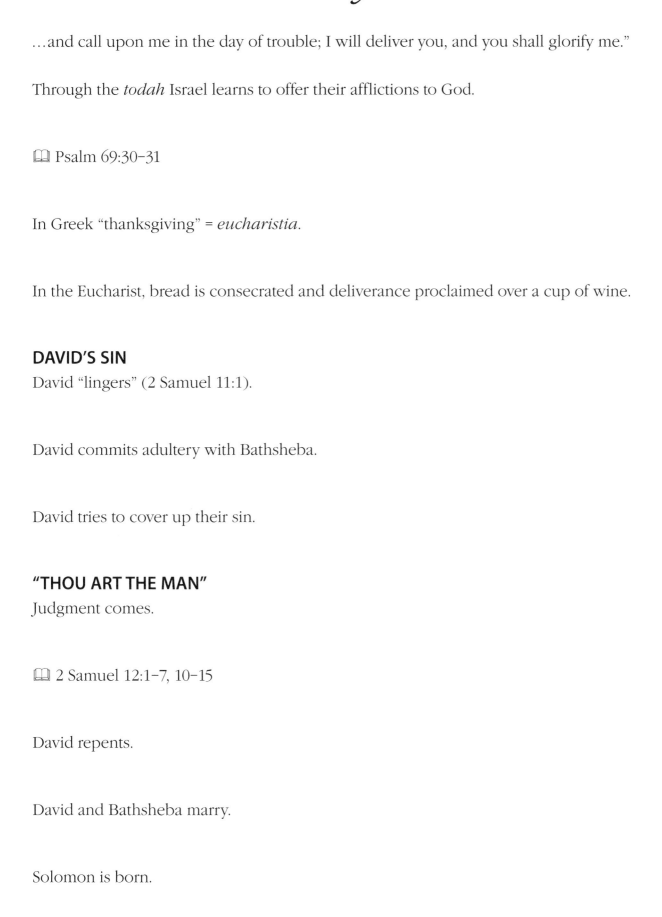

…and call upon me in the day of trouble; I will deliver you, and you shall glorify me."

Through the *todah* Israel learns to offer their afflictions to God.

📖 Psalm 69:30–31

In Greek "thanksgiving" = *eucharistia*.

In the Eucharist, bread is consecrated and deliverance proclaimed over a cup of wine.

DAVID'S SIN

David "lingers" (2 Samuel 11:1).

David commits adultery with Bathsheba.

David tries to cover up their sin.

"THOU ART THE MAN"

Judgment comes.

📖 2 Samuel 12:1–7, 10–15

David repents.

David and Bathsheba marry.

Solomon is born.

FROM MOSES TO DAVID

Moses	David
Sinai/Desert	Zion/Jerusalem
Exclusive/National	Inclusive/International
Tent for Israel's worship	Temple for all to worship
Sin offerings	Thank offerings
Torah: Law of God	*Hokmah*: Wisdom of Solomon

FULFILLING ABRAHAM'S COVENANT

Three promises in Genesis 12, 17, and 22 fulfilled

1. Land and nationhood (1 Kings 4:20-21)

2. Royal dynasty

3. Worldwide blessing

SOLOMON'S LATER FAILURES

Solomon ignores Moses' warnings (Deuteronomy 17:14–17)

Weapons (2 Chronicles 9:25, 28)

Wealth (see 1 Kings 10:14, 23–27)

Wives (1 Kings 11:1–4)

FALL OF THE KINGDOM

930 BC:	The kingdom divides
Ten northern tribes	Two southern tribes
Israel	Judah
722 BC: Destroyed by Assyrians	586 BC: Destroyed by Babylonians seventy-year exile

THE PROPHETS

📖 Isaiah 9:1–7: Restoration will come.

The Messiah will offer himself for the sins of the world (Isaiah 53:5, 10, 12).

God will establish a new covenant.

📖 Jeremiah 31:31–33

QUESTIONS FOR REVIEW

1. What is the twofold role of David? In what way is he both a king and a priest?

2. What are the seven major characteristics of the Davidic covenant? How do these characteristics relate to Christ and his work?

3. What are the three secondary characteristics of the Davidic covenant? How do these point forward to the new covenant?

4. In what ways does God's covenant with David partially fulfill God's covenant with Moses? with Abraham?

5. How do the prophets describe the victory of the coming Messiah?

QUESTIONS FOR DISCUSSION

1. What does "to obey is better than sacrifice" mean?

2. David sinned gravely, but Scripture still describes him as a man "after God's own heart." How can that be? What do you think that phrase means?

3. How does David honor the Lord's anointed one, even when that anointed one is plagued by an evil spirit and attempting to kill him? How could that attitude serve as a model for us?

4. What is David's "near occasion" for sin? Is it simply watching Bathsheba, or did some other sin precede that one? What does that tell us about what it takes to avoid serious sin?

5. What lesson can we learn from the prophets and their insistence that the Messiah would come?

RECOMMENDED VERSES TO MEMORIZE

Jeremiah 31:31–33

Matthew 1:1

Luke 1:32–33

FOLLOW-UP READING AND PREPARATION FOR NEXT LESSON
Matthew 1—7; 16; 24—28

A Father Who Keeps His Promises, chapters 12—13

Lesson Seven

Jesus: Fulfillment of the Promises

INTRODUCTION—THE TIMELINE

CHRIST: THE NEW ADAM IN THE GARDEN

Salvation History Time Line

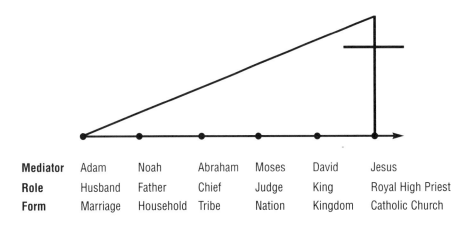

Mediator	Adam	Noah	Abraham	Moses	David	Jesus
Role	Husband	Father	Chief	Judge	King	Royal High Priest
Form	Marriage	Household	Tribe	Nation	Kingdom	Catholic Church

On Easter Sunday the resurrected Christ appears before a woman in a garden (John 20:15).

Jesus prays in the Garden of Gethsemane, "Not as I will, but as thou wilt" (see Luke 22:39–44).

Adam	Christ
Naked and ashamed (Genesis 3:10)	Stripped naked and treated shamefully (Matthew 27:28–29; Hebrews 12:2)
His work brought forth thorns and thistles (Genesis 3:17–18).	Given a crown of thorns (Matthew 27:29)
His labor was hard, sweaty (Genesis 3:19).	Sweats drops of blood (Luke 2:44)
Physical death became inevitable (Genesis 3:19).	Put to death

ON THE THIRD DAY

"And by your descendants shall all the nations of the earth bless themselves" (Genesis 22:18).

THE SON OF ABRAHAM RAISED FROM THE DEAD

Abraham was to sacrifice his only beloved son on Mount Moriah (Genesis 22:2).

Isaac carried the wood for the sacrifice.

Abraham believed "God will provide himself the Lamb" (Genesis 22:8).

Abraham obeyed because of his deep faith (Hebrews 11:19).

Jesus is "the son of Abraham" (Matthew 1:1).

He is the only beloved son of the Father (see Matthew 3:17; John 3:16).

Calvary is one of the peaks of Moriah.

Jesus carries the wood of the sacrifice.

God provides himself *as* the lamb.

God receives his Son back on the third day (Genesis 22:4).

📖 Galatians 3:13–14

BIRTH AND DELIVERANCE

Moses and Jesus

Both are born during the reign of a ruthless king

Ruling tyrants order the murder of Hebrew baby boys.

Both find safety in Egypt.

Both come out of Egypt and pass through the waters and into the desert.

TESTED IN THE DESERT

Fasts for forty days and forty nights

Tested by Satan

Jesus goes right where Israel went wrong.

God will provide (Deuteronomy 8:2–3; Matthew 4:4).

Do not tempt God (Deuteronomy 6:16; Matthew 4:7).

Serve only God (Deuteronomy 6:13; Matthew 4:10).

COVENANT LAW GIVEN ON A MOUNTAIN

Moses descends from Mount Sinai to give Israel the law.

Jesus declares the law of the new covenant from a mountaintop (Matthew 5—7).

"For the law was given through Moses; grace and truth came through Jesus Christ" (John 1:17).

Moses' writings bear witness to Jesus.

📖 John 5:39, 46–47

SIGNS AND MIRACLES

Jesus turns water into wine (John 2:1–11).

Jesus multiplies the loaves (John 6).

📖 John 6:32–35

NEW LEADERS APPOINTED

Jesus appoints twelve apostles and chooses seventy others to assist (Matthew 10:1–8; Luke 10:1).

Moses appointed seventy elders and chose twelve men to enter the Promised Land (Numbers 11; 13).

Jesus' inner circle: Peter, James, and John

Moses' inner circle: Aaron, Nadab, and Abihu

TRANSFIGURED ON A MOUNTAIN

Both Moses and Jesus (Exodus 24:1–15; Luke 9:28–31)

Go up a mountain

With three companions

Covered in glory

Jesus speaks with Moses and Elijah about his exodus.

THE PASSOVER CELEBRATED

"Go and prepare the Passover for us, that we may eat it" (Luke 22:7–13).

"Do this in remembrance of me" (Luke 22:19; Exodus 12:14).

"My blood of the covenant" (Matthew 26:28; Exodus 24:8)

THE PASSOVER FULFILLED

Crucified at the sixth hour (John 19:14)

Jesus is without sin; his legs are not broken (John 19:32–36; Exodus 12:46).

Jesus wears a seamless linen garment (John 19:23).

Hyssop branch (John 19:29; Exodus 12:22–23)

The Eucharist and Christ's death on the cross are the same sacrifice.

Jesus' body "given for you;" Jesus' blood "poured out for you" (Luke 22:19–20)

Levitical priests poured out the blood of the sacrifice (see Exodus 29:12; Leviticus 4:7).

THE RESURRECTION

The Resurrection opens the gates to eternal life (Romans 4:25).

Jesus' humanity is transformed and glorified.

United to him, we share in his glorified humanity.

MATTHEW'S GOSPEL OF THE KINGDOM

Jesus has come to restore the kingdom.

Jesus is the "son of David" (Matthew 1:1).

Jesus was born in the city of David's birth (Matthew 2:5–6; 1 Samuel 16:4).

JESUS THE "CHRIST"

Christ is anointed in the Jordan River by John the Baptist, a Levite.

All the Davidic kings were anointed by Levites (see 1 Kings 1:34; 2 Kings 11:12; 23:30; 2 Chronicles 23:11).

The king was declared a son of God (see Psalm 2:7).

"This is my beloved Son" (see Matthew 3:17).

📖 Matthew 4:23

THE SERMON ON THE MOUNT

The Beatitudes teach the law of the kingdom (Matthew 5:3–10).

We are to pray, "Thy kingdom come" (Matthew 6:9–15).

GREATER THAN SOLOMON

God will provide for our needs even more than he provided for Solomon's (Matthew 6:29, 33).

Jesus' wisdom surpasses that of Solomon.

📖 Matthew 12:42

Both teach through parables (Matthew 13).

ISRAELITES AND GENTILES

Healing of the centurion's son (Matthew 8:5–13)

Proclaiming the kingdom in Tyre and Sidon (Matthew 15:21)

Gentiles fed at the feeding of the four thousand (Matthew 15:31)

THE KEYS OF THE KINGDOM

The kingdom is present through the ministry of the apostles.

Jesus built his Church upon Peter.

📖 Matthew 16:18–19

📖 Isaiah 22:20–22

The prime minister has authority to "open" and "shut" and is a father.

Peter has authority to "open" and "shut."

Pope is derived from the word *Papa*.

Authority resides in the office.

GREATER THAN SOLOMON
Hail the "son of David" (Matthew 21:9).

"Blessed is the kingdom of our father David that is coming" (Mark 11:10).

"Blessed is the King" (Luke 19:38).

Jesus enters riding on a donkey.

📖 1 Kings 1:38–40

THY KINGDOM COME
"I shall not eat it until it is fulfilled in the kingdom of God" (Luke 22:16).

"I shall not drink of the fruit of the vine until the kingdom of God comes" (Luke 22:18).

Eating and drinking when the apostles will sit on thrones in the kingdom (Luke 22:30)

His kingdom won't be like other kingdoms.

📖 Luke 22:24–27

　　　　⌘

In this kingdom... (Luke 22:28–30)

Imitate him

Exercise royal authority

Extend the kingdom...

...through the Eucharist
The only other kingdom covenanted in Scripture is the kingdom of David (Psalm 89:19–37).

THE NEW *TODAH*
Psalm 50:14–15

Step 1: Call out to God for deliverance, and vow to offer a *todah*.

Step 2: Bring a sacrifice to the temple, with bread to be consecrated.

Step 3: Eat the consecrated bread with friends and family, and proclaim God's deliverance.

Todah: Hebrew for "thank offering"

Eucharistia: Greek for "thanksgiving"

Christ prays a *todah* psalm on the cross (Psalm 22).

The Last Supper is a *todah* meal.

Through the Eucharist we share in Christ's *todah*.

THE BOOK OF ACTS

Jesus speaks to the apostles about "the kingdom of God" (Acts 1:3–8).

The apostles are still eager for a kingdom of earthly power.

The kingdom will be restored when they receive the Holy Spirit.

They are to bear witness from Jerusalem, to Judea, to Samaria, "to the ends of the earth" (Psalm 72:8).

DAVIDIC KING ENTHRONED, KINGDOM RESTORED

The Resurrection and Ascension fulfill God's promise to David (Acts 2:29–36).

Peter shows this through Psalms:

Psalm 89:3–4 and Psalm 132:11

Psalm 110:1

THE APOSTLES PREACH THE KINGDOM

Acts begins with Jesus and Peter preaching the kingdom.

The Jerusalem Council: Through the Church the Davidic kingdom is restored.

📖 Acts 15:13–19

Acts ends with Paul preaching the kingdom in Rome (Acts 28:30–31; Romans 1:1–4).

THE HEAVENLY JERUSALEM

Through his resurrection the Redeemer conquers death.

The Davidic king establishes his kingdom forever in heaven (2 Samuel 7:13; Psalm 89:3–4).

📖 Hebrews 12:22–24, 28

"Assembly": *ekklesia*, or church

At the end of the story, the unshakable kingdom is in heaven.

We enter into the kingdom through the Eucharist.

Where the Eucharist is, Christ the King is.

Where the King is, the kingdom is.

Receiving God in the Eucharist is a foretaste of the kingdom.

The Eucharist is life-giving love.

QUESTIONS FOR REVIEW

1. What is the major theme of Jesus' ministry? How does this theme reflect the fulfillment of God's covenant promises in the Old Testament?

2. In what ways does the kingdom restored by Jesus surpass the kingdom of David and Solomon?

3. How is the Eucharist the new Passover? What is the connection between the Passover Jesus celebrates in the Upper Room and the crucifixion?

4. How does Jesus bear the curses Adam and Eve incurred?

5. How does he bear the curse Israel incurred so that God's promise to Abraham can be fulfilled?

QUESTIONS FOR DISCUSSION

1. Read Matthew 13:45–50. What do these two parables tell us about the kingdom of God here on earth?

2. How do we proclaim the kingdom?

3. How is the Eucharist a *todah* sacrifice for us?

4. Read Galatians 2:20. What does it mean to be "crucified with Christ"? What does being "crucified with Christ" have to do with God's covenant promises?

5. Read Hebrews 11. What does this chapter tell us about the purpose of salvation history? What does it tell us about the nature of faith? In what ways can we follow the example of these great witnesses?

RECOMMENDED VERSES TO MEMORIZE

Luke 22:19–20

John 3:16

Acts 1:8

Genesis to Jesus
Review Notes

Lesson 1

Studying Scripture From the Heart of the Church

A Bible Study About the Bible

If we want to understand the Bible, we need to understand its "plot." That plot is salvation history, the story of how God's plan for human salvation unfolds in the course of human events. In order to correctly understand the plot and recognize how Scripture applies to our lives, we need to read the Bible from the heart of the Church, seeing God's story with Catholic eyes. Knowing why we read the Bible and how we should read the Bible can give us that perspective.

The Emmaus Road

Two disciples leave Jerusalem and travel on the road toward Emmaus. They have faith in Jesus but are confused about the events surrounding his crucifixion. Jesus joins them on their journey, but they do not recognize him. They even talk with this "stranger" about Jesus and the events that occurred that very weekend, culminating in the death of Jesus. Then the Lord opens the Scriptures and explains them to the two disciples.

The first thing Jesus does after rising from the dead is to teach his disciples how to read the Scriptures. He explains that the Christ had to suffer and then enter his glory and that all of the Scriptures point to Christ (see Luke 24:26–27). The disciples are amazed yet still do not recognize the stranger walking with them as Jesus.

As the three draw near to Emmaus, the disciples urge Jesus to stay with them. With his consent they sit for a meal. Jesus *takes*, *blesses*, and *breaks* bread; then he *gives* it to his disciples. Immediately this reminds the disciples of Jesus' actions at the Last Supper (see Luke 22:14–20), where he *took*, *blessed*, *broke*, and *gave* bread to his disciples. That was the first celebration of the Mass, where the disciples discovered Christ's real presence in the breaking of the bread.

As soon as the disciples recognize Jesus, he disappears. The disciples are amazed. Now they understand all that Jesus has done with and for them. Immediately they return to Jerusalem.

The Mass: The Key to the Bible

Notice this vital connection: the *reading* of Scripture caused the disciples' *hearts* to burn; the *breaking* of bread caused their *eyes* to be opened (see Luke 24:30–31). Likewise, through the *reading* of Scripture in the Liturgy of the Word and the *breaking* of bread in the Liturgy of the Eucharist, *our* hearts are enflamed and *our* eyes are opened—at every Mass!

Through Jesus the fullness of God's revelation comes to us. The Word of God is revealed both in the Scriptures and in the Eucharist (see *Dei Verbum,* 21). Thus we have a personal encounter with the Word of God in the Mass. We receive the *written* word of God along with the *Eucharistic* Word of God!

The Bible is a liturgical book. Its content is liturgical, and its context is the liturgy. At every stage of God's plan, God's people respond to his covenant love by offering sacrifice and entering into his presence as a worshiping community. The books of the Bible were assembled to be read in the liturgy. The apostles urged believers to read their apostolic letters in church (see Colossians 4:16; 1 Thessalonians 5:27; Revelation 1:3). This is what it means to read the Bible from the heart of the Church.

Many believers through the centuries could not own a copy of the Bible: They lived before any Scripture was written or before the invention of the printing press. However, believers *did* have access to the Scriptures through the readings at Mass.

Likewise the Church gives us the whole Bible to be read at Mass, so that like the early disciples, *our* hearts will burn when we have the Scriptures opened to us. First, we hear Old Testament readings from Moses and the prophets; then we hear New Testament readings, from Jesus and the apostles.

Following the reading and explanation of Scripture, Jesus wants us to receive what the disciples received: *himself.* During the Mass the priest *takes* the bread. The priest then *blesses* the bread with Jesus' very words. He also *breaks* the bread. Finally the priest *gives* the bread to us. Like the disciples, we "recognize" and receive the risen Jesus "in the breaking of bread" (see Luke 24:31, 35).

The Word Incarnate and the Word Written

After Jesus ascends to the Father, the promised Holy Spirit descends upon the disciples at Pentecost. He is the "Spirit of truth" sent to lead the apostles "into all the truth" (John 16:13). How does he do that? The Holy Spirit *inspires* Scripture, *safeguards* the Church's interpretation of the Scripture, and *continues to guide* Jesus' disciples into all truth through the Church.

Dei Verbum states that "the Sacred Scriptures contain the Word of God, and, because they are inspired, they are truly the Word of God" (*Dei Verbum,* 24). This kind of "inspiration" does not refer to artistic creativity as we might understand it. Rather, all Scripture is *theopneustos* [thay ah´ new stos], which means "God-breathed" (see 2 Timothy 3:16).

The Bible, unlike any other book in the entire world, is the Word of God in the very words of God and men. It is divinely inspired, without reducing its human authorship to mechanical dictation. The human authors, moved by the Holy Spirit, wrote the Scriptures (see 2 Peter 1:21), so the sacred books bear the authors' own personal styles and individual perspectives. Since God is the primary Author behind the human authors, everything the Bible teaches is without error (*Dei Verbum,* 11).

The Word is both *divine* and *human*. Just as the Word of God Incarnate took on all the weaknesses of human flesh yet without sin (see Hebrews 4:15), so the Word of God inspired comes to us with all the limitations of human language yet without error. This is why the Church venerates the Word written just as she venerates the Body of Christ.

The Bible is not just one book; it is a book of books. It contains a variety of literature: poetry, prose, prophecy, narrative, proverbs, parables, and more. Its authors exhibit literary artistry, though their backgrounds and educations varied.

Promise and Fulfillment

Unlike the modern secular approach to history, the Bible gives us history from God's perspective: God's Word reveals God's saving work. *Scripture gives us the drama of the history of salvation.*

Structurally the Bible is divided into two parts: the Old Testament and the New Testament. Scripture *begins* with Creation (see Genesis 1:1); it *ends* with the passing away of this world and the coming of a "new heaven" and a "new earth" (see Revelation 21:1). At the *center* of the drama, however, is the *cross* of Jesus (see Galatians 4:4−5). Salvation history is a "two-part" story that presents the world *before* Jesus (the promises of God) and the world *during* and *after* Jesus' life, death, and resurrection (the fulfillment of God's promises).

Scripture is literature, but it is not *just* literature. The words—the "literary signs"—communicate historical realities.

God writes the world as men write words. He gives us signs that stand for realities. He even uses historical realities to represent greater realities. For example, the Exodus events foreshadow Christ's work of redemption.

Throughout the Old Testament God promises his children a savior who will deliver them from their sins. He provides various "saviors," such as Noah, Moses, the judges, King David, and others, who in fact provide a kind of deliverance. God uses them to prefigure *the* Savior.

Throughout the New Testament God reveals the *fulfillment* of his promises. Jesus is *the* Savior of the world who was promised to the Israelites in the Old Testament (see Luke 1:68–79). Jesus commissions his apostles to restore his divine family (see Matthew 28:19–20); in turn the apostles proclaim him to be the fulfillment of God's promises to the fathers (see Acts 13:16–41). They read the Old Testament in light of the New and the New Testament in light of the Old (see, for example, 1 Corinthians 10:1–11).

Furthermore the *Catechism* states that "thanks to the unity of God's plan, not only the text of Scripture but also the realities and events about which it speaks can be signs" (CCC 117). Thus the Old Testament *people* and *events* prefigure and point to the New Testament *Redeemer* and his saving *mysteries*. There are literary clues throughout the Bible that convey the text's meaning.

St. Augustine clarified that the New Testament *lies hidden* in the Old, and the Old Testament is *unveiled* in the New. His insight into the unity of Scripture through this pattern of "concealment-revelation" is known as *typology*. He faithfully taught what the early Church fathers had seen: Christ was foreshadowed in the Old Testament by "types."

The Old Testament *foreshadows* New Testament realities. For example, in the Old Testament an unblemished lamb was offered as a Passover sacrifice; in the New Testament Jesus is the "Lamb of God, who takes away the sin of the world" (John 1:29; see 1 Corinthians 5:7b). Likewise, in the Old Testament the people of Israel ate miraculous bread (called "manna") in the wilderness; in the New Testament Jesus is the Bread of Life, "the true bread from heaven" (see John 6:31–35). Further, Hebrews 10:1 refers to the sacrificial laws, which assisted the people of God in the Old Testament yet were only a shadow of the true form of the reality revealed in Christ's sacrificial offering. Many more examples of typology will follow throughout this study.

Typology "discerns" God's fatherly works in the Old Testament, which point to—and are fulfilled in—*Jesus* in the New Testament (see CCC 128). Typology shows us that the meaning of the events contained in the Old Testament is "inexhaustible" (CCC 129). Further, typology points to the ongoing "dynamic movement" toward the fulfillment of God's fatherly plan (CCC 130).

We are not merely *students* of God's work in the past, nor are we *spectators* of this "dynamic movement" from the outside. Quite the contrary: We intimately *participate* in God's saving plan. In a very real sense, we are standing in the "stream" of salvation history.

The Bible: A Gift From God

The Bible is a family heirloom, passed from generation to generation. It is a treasure to be valued and shared. It was written for the sake of our salvation (see 2 Timothy 3:14–17). In the Scriptures God comes down to our *human* level to raise us up to his *divine* level.

The Bible takes the guesswork out of how we can please God. The Bible expresses the ancient truth that all of life is under the authority of God's Word (see Psalm 119:12–16): family life (see Deuteronomy 6), worship (see Nehemiah 8), and social institutions (see Exodus 20—24).

The Holy Spirit Safeguards Interpretation

St. Paul writes, "So then, brethren, stand firm and hold to the traditions which you were taught by us, either by word of mouth or by letter" (2 Thessalonians 2:15). "Word of mouth" refers to what St. Paul taught the people through oral tradition—through teaching, preaching, and worship. "By letter" refers to what St. Paul wrote to the people. St. Paul binds his hearers to "hold fast" to both *oral* and *written* instruction.

Yet it is not enough to have oral and written instruction; the Word of God must be interpreted as well. Misinterpretation is a real danger (see Ephesians 4:11–14). In the Catholic Church we have not only God's Word but also a faithful interpretation—preserved by the Holy Spirit—of God's Word (2 Peter 1:20–21). Instead of fracturing into thousands of denominations that disagree on many beliefs, we have the deposit of faith, which no one can change. The Holy Spirit empowers the magisterium—the bishop of Rome and the bishops united with him—to serve the people of God by faithfully preserving and proclaiming the full revelation of God (see CCC 100).

"Sacred Tradition and sacred Scripture make up a single sacred deposit of the Word of God" (*Dei Verbum,* 10). Tradition is alive because it is the faithful handing down of revelation from Christ, through the apostles' preaching and writing. It is living and dynamic, especially in the

liturgy. The Scriptures are also living and dynamic (see Hebrews 4:12). Though there were many human authors of Scripture, there is one primary Author, God, who is the Source of that unity. We must trust the same Holy Spirit who inspired Sacred Scripture to empower the Church to interpret it (see Ephesians 1:9–10).

The great early Church father St. Irenaeus recognized the need for studying salvation history in terms of covenants. "Understanding…consists in…showing why there are a number of covenants with mankind, and in teaching what is the character of each of the covenants" (*Against Heresies*, book 1, chapter 10, no. 3).

Salvation History Is Covenant History

The Old and New Testaments point to the old and new covenants (what we call "testament," ancient Israelites called "covenant"). The story of salvation is recorded as a sequence of covenants that God makes with his people.

Most people think that a covenant is the same thing as a contract. This is *not* true: Covenants are *much more* than mere contracts. Covenants and contracts both establish *relationships*, but the *types* of relationships they establish are very different.

Contracts are made with a *promise*; covenants are sworn with an *oath*. Contracts are signed in *our* name; covenants are sealed in *God's* name. Contracts exchange *goods and services*; covenants exchange *persons*. Contracts are *temporary*; covenants are *permanent*.

Covenants establish the strongest type of interpersonal communion: family or kinship bonds. In short, the difference between a *covenant* and a *contract* is about as significant as that between *marriage* and *prostitution*!

A covenant is a sacred family bond in which persons give themselves to one another in loving communion. God's covenants establish us as his family (see Ezekiel 36:28). He is our heavenly Father because of his covenant with us (see CCC 238). We will examine in this Bible study a series of covenants God established with his family.

The first covenant was made with *Adam and Eve* as *husband and wife*. The second covenant was made with *Noah*, who was the head of a *household*. The third covenant was made with *Abraham*, who was the *chieftain* of an extensive *tribe*. The fourth covenant was made with *Moses*, who was *judge* over the *nation* of the twelve tribes of Israel. The fifth covenant was made with *King David*, who ruled the *kingdom* of Israel.

And finally *Jesus* establishes the new covenant, the worldwide (catholic) kingdom of God. Salvation history reaches its goal in Christ: All things are united to him (see Ephesians 1:10). This covenant invites all people to be received into the family of God through the Catholic Church, so that all nations will be restored into his divine covenantal family through and in Jesus Christ.

Salvation history is not a thing of the past: It is still unfolding. We are still in the "flow" of salvation history. The rest of the study will examine God's plan for salvation and our place in it.

Lesson 2
The Creation Covenant

In the Beginning

In Genesis 1:1–2 we read about God calling the world into existence. Not only does he create the world, but he also establishes a covenant with his creation. Jeremiah 33:25 refers to God's "covenant with day and night." God did not create us because he was lonely or bored; as Father, Son, and Holy Spirit, he created us to be his family.

Many people approach Genesis 1 and 2 in terms of a "religion versus science" debate. They often forget to read the text as the ancients would have read it. If readers impose current questions and historical situations on the text of Scripture, they miss the whole point of the account.

Genesis 1 was not written to tell us *how* the world was created. Rather it was written to tell us *what* was created and *why* it was created. Creation was the deliberate, purposeful act of a loving God. The Catholic Church teaches that we are not bound to believe either that God created the earth in six twenty-four-hour days or he used evolution. However, the Church teaches that we must believe that God created the world, that he created our first parents, and that they existed with him for a time in a state of original justice, happiness, and innocence before their fall into sin.

In the Creation account God says, "Let there be …," and things come into being (Genesis 1:3, 6, 14). God does what he says; when he speaks, things happen. Creation occurs because of God's word (see Psalm 33:6–9). Reading the Old Testament in light of the New, we know that Jesus is the Word of God by which the world was created (see John 1:1–3; Colossians 1:16–17; Hebrews 1:2).

Genesis 1:2 states that in the beginning the world was "without form and void." God changes this: He gives the world forms (*realms*) and fills the void (with *rulers*). After each day God declares that his work is "good" (1:4, 10, 18, 21, 25). But after the *sixth* day, the day of creating mankind, God declares that his work is "very good" (1:31).

Genesis 1:26–27 states that humans are made in the "image and likeness" of God. What does this mean? We find a literary clue in Genesis 5:1–3: Adam was made in the likeness of God, and Adam's son, Seth, was made in Adam's "own likeness, after his image." We can conclude from this that *image* and *likeness* refer to sonship. Thus Adam was "the son of God" (Luke 3:38).

The Sabbath

After God creates man and woman, the Scriptures tell us, he ordains the day of rest (see Genesis 2:2). Upon first glance, this day of rest can be a little perplexing. Does the all-powerful God *need* to rest? No, he is not tired. The seventh day finishes God's design for creation. God blesses and hallows the seventh day to give us a gift—a holy day of *rest* from our labor and a call to *worship* him as members of his covenant family (see Genesis 15:5; Jeremiah 33:19–26; CCC 288).

The seventh day seals God's covenant with creation. He swears a covenant oath. The Hebrew word for swearing an oath is *sheba* [sheh vah´], which literally means "to seven oneself." God "sevens" time into seven days to consecrate creation. The Sabbath is a perpetual covenant (see Exodus 31:16–17).

God's Sabbath is the climax of the Creation account. Through it God calls man and woman to something far more glorious than "ruling" creation: God calls them to interpersonal communion with him. The world is not just a place of work; it is also a place of *worship*, a holy dwelling place where God himself is present, where his people worship and offer sacrifice.

Scripture describes Creation as the building of a home or temple (see Job 38:4–11). Solomon builds the temple in seven years and consecrates it in the seventh month, on the seventh day of a seven-day feast, offering seven petitions (see 1 Kings 6—8). In the temple the Holy of Holies is truly the dwelling place of God; the Garden of Eden is described in terms similar to those describing the inner precincts of the temple (see Genesis 2:2–14). Once God completes the temple of the world, he calls man to be a priest-king over it.

Two Creation Accounts

Genesis 1 and 2 record two accounts of Creation. These are not two conflicting accounts; they are complementary accounts with different emphases.

In Genesis 1 God the *Creator* makes a cosmic home or temple for himself. His final creation—man and woman—he makes in his image, and he calls them to imitate him (see verse 28). In Genesis 2 God works as *Father*. He lovingly fashions man from the dirt of the earth, breathes life into him, creates a garden paradise for him, and creates a spouse for him from his very side. God commands man to "till…and keep" the garden (Genesis 2:15), a call to priestly sacrifice in the garden sanctuary.

Adam is God's royal firstborn son, the high priest of humanity. In ancient Israel the father, as head of his family, was a priest who offered sacrifices and performed acts of worship on behalf of his household. This priesthood was passed down from father to firstborn son, who inherited the mantle of the authority of the family to lead the people to be holy. Jesus—as the "new Adam" (Romans 5:14)—calls his people, the Church, to be a "holy nation" and a "royal priesthood" (1 Peter 2:9; see Revelation 1:6).

Not only does God create man and woman in a covenant relationship with him, but he also creates them in covenant union with each other. They are joined as one in the covenant of marriage. God establishes marriage as a sign of his covenant love for us.

In a very real sense, the Trinity is the divine family, and the image of the Triune God is reflected in our natural families. More than a sign, marriage is an image of who God is.

Temptation and Fall: Making Sense of the Story

The *Catechism* gives us three important things to remember when examining man's temptation and fall: (1)"The account of the fall in Genesis 3 uses figurative language"; (2)"but [the account] affirms a primeval event, a deed that took place *at the beginning of the history of man*" (see *Gaudium et Spes* 13 §1); (3) "revelation gives us the certainty of faith that the whole of human history is marked by the original fault freely committed by our first parents" (see Council of Trent: DS 1513; Pius XII: DS 3897; Paul VI: AAS 58 [1966], 654) (CCC, 390). Though the account in Genesis 3 is written more like poetry than journalism, it affirms an actual event—the "original fault" of Adam and Eve—that forever marks human history.

From the very beginning God alerts Adam and his helpmate Eve that there is a *danger*. Adam should "keep" or guard the garden (see Genesis 2:15); this implies that there is something to guard against! God also gives Adam a *limitation* or *restriction*: Adam can eat of every tree of the garden except one (see Genesis 2:16–17). Furthermore, God gives Adam a *warning*: If Adam disobeys and eats of the forbidden tree, he will die that day (see Genesis 2:17). Death has to be meaningful (understood) and dreadful (fearing the loss of life), or the boundary would have been meaningless to Adam.

When God breathes life into Adam, he gives him more than he gave any other creature: God gives Adam the grace of divine sonship. He gives Adam *natural life* and *supernatural life.*

Adam and Eve are created in a state of grace (see CCC 375). They live in harmony with God, with each other, and with all of creation. They are not prone to sin, nor are they simple-minded

or inadequate to the test God gives them. Quite the contrary: They are intelligent and upright people who live in right relationship with God.

Along Came a Serpent

We've all seen Bible story images of a long, thin snake slithering around an apple tree. It is important to note, however, that the Hebrew word for "serpent" is *nahash* [nuh hawsh?], which is a much more dangerous animal than the garden-variety snake. *Nahash* refers to an extremely deadly and dangerous creature (see, for example, Numbers 21:6–9; Isaiah 27:1–3; Revelation 12:3, 9). Once we see the nature of the serpent that confronts Adam and Eve, we see the serious challenge and grave threat Adam faces in guarding the garden and his wife (see CCC 395).

The Serpent speaks to Eve, but he addresses Adam also. (The Hebrew word for "you" is plural.) The Serpent directly contradicts God's solemn warning to Adam about the forbidden fruit: "You will not die" (Genesis 3:4). This temptation is a test.

Adam's test involves four questions: (1) As a *son*, will Adam trust God as Father enough to obey? (2) As *king*, will Adam exercise dominion over the beasts and drive the Serpent out of the garden? (3) As *husband*, will Adam protect his bride? (4) As *priest*, will Adam—if need be— offer his life in a sacrifice of love and obedience? In short, will Adam fear a loss of *supernatural life* more than a loss of *natural* human life?

Adam fails the test: He does not trust in his heavenly Father. He fails to guard the garden, and the Serpent gains entrance. Further, Adam is *silent* when he should speak. Then Adam allows his wife to lead him into sin, instead of leading her into righteousness. Finally, Adam refuses to offer himself to God; he prefers himself to his Creator (see CCC 397–398).

God Confronts Adam and Eve

God comes to Adam and Eve in the garden, not in a leisurely stroll but in judgment. They hear the powerful "sound" of the Lord (see Genesis 3:8; Psalm 29:1–9), and they are afraid. Instead of running to the Lord, they hide.

In Genesis 3:9–13 God asks Adam and Eve four questions: (1) "Where are you?" (2) "Who told you that you were naked?" (3) "Have you eaten of the tree of which I commanded you not to eat?" (4) "What is this that you have done?" (3:8–13).

The all-powerful and all-knowing God surely knows the answers to these questions. But he wants Adam and Eve to face the reality of the grave sin they have committed. He gives them every chance to confess their sins and to be reconciled to him. Rather than facing their sin, however, Adam and Eve make excuses and blame others—even God (3:12–13).

God turns to the source of the trouble: the Serpent. He *curses* the Serpent with humiliation and destruction. God also *prophesies enmity* between the Serpent and the woman, between his offspring and hers (see Genesis 3:14–15).

God then tells man and woman the consequences of their sin. Childbirth will be painful. Relationships will be marred by sin. Work will be toil; it will not always be fruitful and instead will bring forth thorns and thistles. Even the ground will be cursed. Finally, physical death will be inevitable for all (see Genesis 3:16–19).

While Adam and Eve don't die physically in the garden, they do die spiritually. That day they lose God's divine life in their souls. This spiritual death is far worse than any physical death. This is the original mortal sin: the "death of the soul" (CCC 403; see Council of Trent: DS 1512).

Adam and Eve lose their innocence and intimacy with God. Furthermore, their harmony with each other and with creation is lost. Seduced into trying to be like God without God, they exercise freedom that plunges them—and us—into slavery and death (see CCC 398). They discover their nakedness and are ashamed.

God shows mercy to Adam and Eve. He covers their nakedness by making them garments out of animal skins, thus making the first sacrifice of animals to cover the shame of his children. Then he drives them out of the garden, and he posts cherubim at the entrance so that they will not be tempted to reenter and seal their damnation by eating of the Tree of Everlasting Life (see Genesis 3:21–22).

The First Gospel

God does not give up on his fallen son and daughter, however. He promises a Redeemer who will save his children, who will set right the wrong of Adam and Eve. The early Church fathers understood this promise as the "first gospel" (or the *protoevangelium*) (see CCC 410). The Fathers also understood the "seed of the woman" to be a reference to the Virgin Birth, since "seed" (*spermatos*) comes from the man rather than the woman.

God's promise of a Redeemer is the promise of a "New Adam" and a "New Eve" who will do what the first Adam and Eve failed to do (and undo what the first couple did) (see CCC 410–411). The *New Adam* will be the one who will achieve victory over the Serpent. The *New Eve* will be his mother, the one who gives birth to the Redeemer. Just as death comes into the human race through the sin of the first Adam and Eve, so new life will come through the victory of the New Adam and the New Eve, Jesus and Mary (see Romans 5:17–19; 1 Corinthians 15:21–22, 45–49).

Sin enters the world through the "fear of death" (Hebrews 2:14–15), for Adam fears natural death over supernatural death. In contrast, Jesus takes our human nature so that through his death he can destroy the devil, who has the power of death. Jesus' death, then, delivers all of us from lifelong bondage to sin, to which we succumb because of the fear of death.

Jesus bears the curses of the covenant as the New Adam. He goes into a garden (see Matthew 26:36–46), and his sweat is like drops of blood (see Luke 22:44). However, unlike the first Adam, Jesus faces the fears of suffering and death; he chooses to trust his heavenly Father: "Father, if thou art willing, remove this chalice from me; nevertheless not my will, but yours, be done" (Luke 22:42).

Jesus' crown of thorns (see Matthew 27:29) harkens back to the thorns and thistles of Adam's fate. Like Adam and Eve, Jesus is reduced to nakedness (see Matthew 27:28, 31, 35). Jesus dies on the cross, which was referred to as the "Tree of Life" in the early Church (see Acts 5:30). Finally, falling into the sleep of death, his Bride—the Church—is formed from his side (see John 19:34).

Jesus gives us the perfect example of total self-offering when he lays down his life for us on the cross. Unlike the first Adam, Jesus yields his will completely in trust to his heavenly Father. He lays down his life for his Bride, the Church. Through the Last Adam, what was lost through the sin of the first Adam is restored. Even more, we can now become partakers of the divine nature, since we have been given Jesus' divine life.

Church tradition has always seen Mary as "the New Eve." In contrast to the first Eve's disregard of God's commands, Mary offers herself freely to the will of God: "Behold, I am the handmaid of the Lord; let it be to me according to your word" (Luke 1:38).

The story of the Bible is the story of God's love for his people. Just as Adam and Eve are united in marriage on the seventh day, so God wants to be united to his people in a "nuptial" or marriage-like (covenantal) bond.

We hardly can grasp God's love for us in human language. So here, in the first pages of the Bible, the Word of God uses the most powerful images of human love imaginable—that of parent and child, that of husband and wife.

Covenant love requires total self-giving: God gives himself to his people, and his people give themselves to him. This kind of love images the life-giving love of the Trinity. And since God destined us to share in his divine life, we need to learn to love as he does. From him we learn how to give ourselves fully—how to sacrifice ourselves—for each other and, most importantly, for him.

We can say that the Bible tells the story of God's raising us as his family from infancy to adulthood. Little by little he guides us, chastises us, woos us, and prepares us to be fit for the wedding supper of the Lamb of heaven. He calls us to divine, heavenly union with him, which can be symbolized best by marriage—the most ecstatic and intimate of human relationships.

This is our heavenly calling, our supernatural end.

Lesson 3

Noah and a Renewed Creation

Cain's Sin

In the last lesson we looked at the first covenant in salvation history, the covenant in Creation with Adam and Eve. Though the sin of Adam and Eve sent humanity into a downward spiral of wickedness, God did not abandon the human family. God promised redemption through Christ "when the time had fully come" (Galatians 4:4). It is only in Christ that God's covenant plan for creation is fulfilled at last.

As forewarned in Genesis 3:15, throughout human history there is ongoing conflict between the two seeds, the seed of the *woman* (righteousness) and the seed of the *Serpent* (wickedness). Adam and Eve have children after God expels them from his presence; immediately the "enmity" between the two seeds becomes evident in their sons.

From the beginning of time, people have come into God's presence to worship through sacrifice. Adam and Eve's sons—Cain and Abel—do this. God accepts Abel's sacrifice (see Hebrews 11:4), but he has no regard for Cain's offering (see 1 John 3:11). This greatly angers Cain.

God warns Cain to guard his heart, to resist the temptation that is trying to master him. Tragically, however, Cain defies God, gives in to envy, and murders his brother (see Genesis 4:7–8).

Just as God confronted Adam and Eve after the Fall, he questions Cain in order to bring him to repentance. Like his parents, Cain has excuses. He refuses to confess, and he goes on to accuse *God* and others of injustice (see Genesis 4:13–14).

Previously God cursed the Serpent and the ground but not the humans involved, not Adam and Eve (see Genesis 3:14–19). Now God curses Cain (see Genesis 4:10–12). The ground will not yield fruit because he has defiled it by soaking it with the innocent blood of his brother. Furthermore, Cain is driven "east" of Eden, to be a fugitive in the land of Nod (which means "wandering"). Banished and ostracized, Cain has made himself a marked man (see Genesis 4:14).

God's covenant curses are not done out of divine mean-spiritedness. A covenant curse is an extreme form of fatherly punishment, designed to lead hardened sinners to repentance. God

answers Cain's dismay with the promise, "If any one slays Cain, vengeance shall be taken on him sevenfold" (Genesis 4:15). This illustrates what has always been true: God doesn't punish us because he stops loving us; he punishes us because he *can't* stop loving us!

Adam's Family Divided

Following the loss of Abel in death and Cain in banishment, Adam and Eve have another son, Seth. Through Seth a righteous family line develops. The two seeds and sons—Cain's and Seth's—now emerge as two family lines in conflict.

Cain and the Wicked Line. Cain has a son and names him Enoch. Cain builds a city and names it after his son. The fact that Cain names a city after his son is evidence of his desire to glorify himself.

Seven generations from Adam, we see the full flowering of evil in Cain's line. Lamech—a descendant of Cain—takes two wives. He violates God's plan for the marriage covenant in creation through bigamy. He is also defiant, violent, vengeful, and murderous (see Genesis 4:19, 23–24).

Seth and the Righteous Line. Through Seth's family, proper worship is restored. They "called upon the name (*shem*) of the Lord" (Genesis 4:26). Here *shem* refers to God's glory rather than one's own. This phrase refers elsewhere to sacrificial worship (see Genesis 12:8).

In the seventh generation from Adam we see the full flowering of righteousness in Enoch. The descendant of Seth has a close relationship with God (see Genesis 5:24; Hebrews 11:5). Thus the image and likeness of God in Adam—divine sonship—is renewed with Seth and his family line (see Genesis 5).

Genesis 6 intimates, however, that the Sethite line is compromised through mixed marriages with the women of Cain's family. Seduced by their beauty, the Sethites (the "sons of God") enter into illicit unions with the Cainite women, "the daughters of men" (Genesis 6:2). The wicked fruit of these mixed marriages are men of great pride and extreme violence. They are called "the men of renown" (Genesis 6:4)—literally, "the men of the name (*shem*)." Here again *shem* refers to the pursuit of glory, but it is their own glory rather than God's. The offspring of these mixed marriages fall away from the covenant and embrace wickedness (see Genesis 6:5–6).

Saved Through Water

The wickedness of humanity reaches its pinnacle in Genesis 6:5. Noah alone "walked with God" (Genesis 6:9).

This state of affairs provokes God to pronounce severe judgment. He chooses righteous Noah to serve as the covenant mediator between God and the people. Thus Noah and his household form a righteous remnant through whom God will bring about a new beginning. God instructs Noah to build the ark in order to save his family as well as representatives of every beast and bird.

Noah responds in obedience. By faith "Noah…did all that God commanded him" (Genesis 6:22; see Hebrews 11:7). Noah bears witness to a wicked generation of God's impending judgment (the Flood) and his covenant mercy (the ark).

The Hebrew word for covenant, *berith* [beh-reet´], is first used in Genesis 6:18. The Hebrew statement that God will establish his covenant implies a renewal of a previous covenant. Thus God is not doing something radically new or different; he is promising to renew the covenant of Creation. He wants to renew his covenant with Noah's household.

There are several significant parallels between the Flood narrative (see Genesis 6—8) and the Creation account (see Genesis 1—2). In both narratives a new world emerges from the waters of "the deep" (see Genesis 1:2; 7:11). The number seven recurs in both accounts: Noah and his family board the ark and wait *seven* days before the Flood begins (see Genesis 7:10); the ark rests in the *seventh* month (see Genesis 8:4); Noah sends out birds every *seven* days (see Genesis 8:10–12); Noah takes *seven* pairs of "clean animals" (animals acceptable for sacrifice) into the ark (see Genesis 7:2).

Additionally, Noah's name means "rest" or "relief" (see Genesis 5:29), reflecting the seventh-day Sabbath mandate. The Sabbath is the sign of God's covenant with creation; the rainbow becomes the sign of God's renewed covenant with creation.

In the last lesson we saw how God established a covenant with Adam as *husband*. In this lesson we see how God renews his covenant with Noah as *husband*. Even more than husband, however, God renews his covenant with Noah as *father of a household*. There are four married couples on the ark, and Noah is the head of the covenant family.

Thus God renews his covenant with Noah, his family, and all creation through sacrifice and worship (see Genesis 8:20–22; 9:8, 17). Noah was called to "re-found" God's covenant family, like a new Adam. Just as there are parallels between the Flood and Creation, so there are significant parallels between Noah and Adam.

Like Adam, Noah is told to "be fruitful and multiply, and fill the earth" (Genesis 1:28; 9:1). Like Adam, Noah is given dominion over the creatures of the earth (see Genesis 1:28; 9:2). Both Adam and Noah find themselves in a garden or vineyard (see Genesis 2:15; 9:20). Both Adam and Noah consume fruit that expose their nakedness (see Genesis 3:6–7; 9:21). And even after the Fall, both still bear the image of God (see Genesis 1:26; 9:6).

God's covenant with Noah renews divine sonship, restores royal dominion, and resumes priestly sacrifice. But just as Adam's family divided into godly and ungodly lines, so does Noah's family.

The Table of Nations

Genesis 10 contains Noah's genealogy, identifying seventy descendants who founded the nations of the ancient world. This "table of nations" is absolutely unique: No other ancient genealogy portrays the entire human race as one worldwide family. It reveals God's fatherly perspective and purpose for humanity. It shows how the original unity of the human family in Adam is restored in Noah. It also demonstrates the ongoing pattern of human sin and divine judgment.

The table of nations helps the people of God understand their place in the world. It shows the righteous line, the descendants of Shem and Eber, who they are: bearers of God's blessing to the human race.

Through Noah's faithful firstborn son, Shem, God continues to build his covenant family. As we have seen, *shem* is also the word used for "name"—the term for "glory" and "fame." While the wicked pursue their own vainglory, Shem's righteous line seeks to advance the glory of God.

Ancient Israel traces its national origin back to the righteous descendants of Noah who bear the blessing: Shem and Eber. Shem's ancestors are called "Semites." Eber (from whom we get the word *Hebrew*) is the great-grandson of Shem. The children of Eber are the ancestors of Abraham, Isaac, and Israel (see Genesis 11:10–26).

Conversely, the unrighteous line of Ham is the source of moral corruption and conflict. In fact, the rest of Old Testament history records the ongoing suffering of Israel at the hands of Ham's wicked descendants. Ham's line reads like a Who's Who list of Israel's enemies: Egyptians, Canaanites, Philistines, Assyrians, and Babylonians (see Genesis 10:6–20; see *A Father Who Keeps His Promises*, p. 90).

The conflict between the lines of Shem and Ham first surfaces during the building of the Tower of Babel in Genesis 11. The wicked people of the earth know that God once destroyed the earth with a flood. And like the people of that time, the descendants of Noah fall into sin and bring down God's judgment.

They begin construction of a tower, an ancient temple, wishing to establish their own fame. They want to make a *shem* for themselves (see Genesis 11:4). They oppose the line of the righteous son, Shem. (Notice how this story is placed in between two genealogies of Shem, Genesis 10:21–32 and 11:10–32.)

The *Catechism* states that through the "perversion of paganism," fallen humanity is "united only in its perverse ambition to forge its own unity as at Babel" (see Wisdom 10:5; Genesis 11:46). It states that the ungodly committed the sins of "polytheism and the idolatry of the nation and of its rulers" (CCC 57).

At Babel God again brings judgment, this time confusing the people's language. They are scattered to the four corners of the earth.

God's covenant with Noah is far-reaching. Though sin shatters the human race into separate peoples, God extends his providential care to the nations. He extends his covenant with Noah to "all flesh that is upon the earth" (Genesis 9:17). "The covenant with Noah remains in force during the times of the Gentiles, until the universal proclamation of the Gospel" (CCC 58; see Genesis 9:13, 16; Luke 21:24; *Dei Verbum* 3).

The covenant with Noah points us to the sacrament of baptism (see 1 Peter 3:20–21). The Flood is a type of baptism. Like the Flood, baptism cleanses us and destroys sin. Furthermore, as a kind of new creation appeared through the waters of destruction, those who are baptized are new creations in Christ.

We also receive a similar warning: Just as Noah's son Ham was saved on the ark but did evil and received a curse rather than a blessing, so baptism places us in a state of grace that needs to be maintained (see CCC 701, 1219, 1269). As in the days of Noah, many in the world today have rejected the Lord. We need to devote ourselves to our sacrificial worship, as Noah and the righteous line of Seth did.

Literary Framework of Genesis 1—11

At first glance the multiple genealogies in Genesis may seem like superfluous information. However, a closer look at these sections reveals the literary artistry of Genesis.

The various stories of Genesis are connected through the use of the Hebrew word for "generations," *toledoth* [to´ leh dote]. Genesis 2:4 introduces the history of the human family by saying, "These are the generations [*toledoth*] of the heavens and the earth." The same term advances the story through the lines of Noah and the patriarchs: "This is the book of the generations of Adam" (Genesis 5:1); and "These are the generations of Noah" (Genesis 6:9).

The repetition of *generations* points to a deliberate literary framework. The term is used *ten times* in Genesis to introduce key figures in salvation history. It reveals the narrative plot of the history of God's family. History is not just about wars, politics, and economics; it is the story of the human race as the family of God.

The author of Genesis links Adam and Eve to Noah, Abraham, and the rest of salvation history. We see this literary structure in the first eleven chapters of Genesis. It reveals that salvation history is shaped by spiritual conflict between the godly and the ungodly, that righteousness and wickedness travel down family lines, and that God vindicates his family and judges those who corrupt it.

From Adam to Noah there are ten generations (see Genesis 5). The wicked of these generations can trace their lineage back to Cain. At the end of the ten generations, God sends judgment on the world in the form of a flood.

Noah has three sons: Shem, Japheth, and Ham. Shem receives the blessing of the firstborn. Ham's descendant Canaan brings forth the wicked of the post-Flood world. From Shem to Terah there are ten generations. Then God sends judgment on the Tower of Babel. Terah has three sons: Abram, Nahor, and Haran. Abram receives the blessing from God.

In the past two lessons we have looked at the conflict within the human family, a conflict between two *seeds* (see Genesis 3:15), two *sons* (see Genesis 4—5; 10), and two *lines* (the *righteous* and the *unrighteous*). In his famous work *The City of God,* St. Augustine understood

Genesis in terms of two cities: the City of God, which is based upon the love of God even to the point of the contempt of self, and the City of Man, which is based upon the love of self even to the point of the contempt of God. Certainly we find ourselves facing a challenge: How do we live as citizens of the City of God while sojourning in the City of Man?

Lesson 4
Abraham: Our Father in Faith

And God Blessed Them...

From the beginning God pronounced his blessing on creation (see Genesis 1:22, 28; 2:3). Life—both the gift of life itself and life-giving power ("be fruitful and multiply")—reveals God's blessing. The blessing of the covenant is given and received through the family. In fact, both natural life and covenant blessing are shared within the family and are part of the family legacy.

Genesis shows how the blessing passes from father to son. After the Flood God restores the blessing through Noah (see Genesis 9:1). Noah then blesses his firstborn son, Shem (see Genesis 9:26). Through Shem, Noah's family receives God's blessing (see Genesis 9:27).

When humanity rejects God, attempting unity without God at the Tower of Babel, God scatters those who are in rebellion (see Genesis 11). Later he promises to bless Abraham for his obedience and through him restore humanity (see Genesis 12).

In Genesis 12:1–3 God uses the term *bless* or *blessing* five times. The divine blessing is transmitted through family lines (that is, Abraham's descendants). Furthermore, humanity will not be united through making a name for itself; only through God will Abraham's name—his *shem*—be made great (see Genesis 12:2). Thus the covenant blessing passed on through Shem will now come through his descendant, Abraham.

From Adam to Noah, God expanded his family from two people to a larger family. Now God expands his family even further: Whereas Noah was the *father* of a *household*, Abraham is the head of an extended family, the *chieftain* of a *tribe*.

Adam triggered the covenant curses through his disobedience; Abraham secures God's blessing through his righteousness. Thus in *Abraham* the failure of Adam is partially reversed, and through his *seed* God promises to bless all humanity again. In Genesis 12:1–3 God promises Abram three things: *land* and *nationhood* (see 12:1–2), a *dynastic kingdom* (see 12:2, "a great name"), and a *worldwide family* (see 12:3). Eventually God strengthens Abraham's faith by upgrading his threefold promise with three covenant oaths (see Genesis 15, 17, 22).

Abram Responds in Faith

When God calls Abram (meaning "exalted father"), Abram is seventy-five years old. He is extremely wealthy but has no heir (see Genesis 12:4–5; 13:2; 16:1). At God's command Abram leaves his home for a nomadic life with part of his clan: his wife Sarai, his nephew Lot, and many domestic servants and their families (see Genesis 12:4–9). Abram is already demonstrating that he is a man of faith (see Hebrews 11:8)! Later God renames him Abraham, which means "father of a multitude" (Genesis 17:4–5).

However, Abraham's life reveals that the road to blessing is paved with trials and temptations. He faces a multitude of hardships, including famine (see Genesis 12:10), exile and temporary "loss" of his wife (see Genesis 12:10–20), family strife and division (see Genesis 13), wars (see Genesis 14:1–16), unfulfilled promises (see Genesis 15), marital discord (see Genesis 16), surgery (circumcision) (see Genesis 17), the supernatural destruction of Sodom and Gomorrah (see Genesis 18:16—19:29), more family strife and division (see Genesis 21:8–21), and the ultimate trial of a father, the offering of his beloved son (see Genesis 22:1–19). Abraham grows in faith through these tests, and he makes ever greater sacrifices.

In the midst of his trials, God fulfills his promise to bless Abram (see Genesis 14:17–20). Abram defeats his enemies; then he meets Melchizedek, whose name means "righteous King," of Salem (Hebrew for "peace"). More than just a king, Melchizedek is a *priest* of God Most High. Melchizedek offers bread and wine to Abram, and then he gives God's blessing to Abram. Abram's response is one of homage in paying him tithes. In short, Melchizedek prefigures Christ in three ways: (1) he is a priest-king who (2) offers bread and wine and (3) receives homage.

Three Promises Strengthened by Three Oaths

In Genesis 12 God makes three promises to Abram: *a nation with its own land* (see Genesis 12:2), *kingship* (a great name, a royal dynasty) (see Genesis 12:2), and *worldwide blessing* (see Genesis 12:3). God rewards Abram's faith with three covenant *oaths*, recorded in Genesis 15, 17, and 22.

The First Covenant Oath. In Genesis 15 Abram is still childless. When God promises him a great reward (see verse 1), Abram respectfully reminds God, *what good is a reward if he has no son to inherit it?* In response God swears a covenant oath to give Abram a son. God makes a covenant with him by passing between the parts of animals cut in two by Abram (see 15:7–21).

The first blessing that God had promised Abram in Genesis 12:2, land and nationhood, is upgraded to a covenant oath. God swears that Abram will be a father to innumerable descendants, who will be delivered from bondage and receive the Promised Land (see Genesis 15:13–16). This foreshadows not only the Hebrews' slavery but also their exodus from Egypt.

As time goes by, however, elderly Abram and his wife, Sarai, grow impatient. They decide to take matters into their own hands. Sarai tells Abram that he should take her Egyptian hand-maid, Hagar, and have a son through her (see Genesis 16:1–3). Abram complies. However, after Hagar conceives a son, she begins to look at Sarai "with contempt," sowing seeds of family discord (see Genesis 16:4).

The Second Covenant Oath. At this point God renames Abram "Abraham," meaning "father of a multitude" (Genesis 17:5). He also renames Sarai "Sarah," meaning "great mother" (Genesis 17:15). God swears another covenant oath to Abraham, to give him a son through his wife Sarah; Ishmael is *not* the chosen heir. God gives an amazing promise: Not just descendants but "kings of peoples shall come from [Sarah]" (Genesis 17:16). This prefigures the covenant God made with David to establish his kingdom, in 2 Samuel 7:9.

God promises that Abraham will have a son in one year through Sarah (see Genesis 17:21). The promise includes a command, however: Abraham must circumcise himself and all the males in his tribe (see Genesis 17:10–14). Ishmael is thirteen years old and is circumcised, as are all the household slaves. From this day forth all descendants of Abraham shall be circumcised on the eighth day.

At this point Abraham is ninety-nine years old. He has three months to recover and conceive with his wife Sarah! Even in his obedience to be circumcised, Abraham demonstrates great faith.

Just as God promised, Isaac is born one year later. After Isaac is weaned, Abraham has a great feast (see Genesis 21:8). Fearful that Ishmael may try to usurp Isaac, Sarah asks Abraham to banish Hagar and Ishmael once and for all from their midst (see Genesis 21:10). Abraham hesitates, until the Lord instructs him to do as Sarah requests.

The Final Covenant Oath. Once Ishmael is banished, Abraham is left with his only beloved son Isaac. Years pass before God gives Abraham the ultimate test: He asks Abraham to sacrifice his son on a mountain of Moriah (see Genesis 22:1–2).

Abraham obeys immediately. He prepares the supplies himself, and he sets off with Isaac on the three-day journey (see Genesis 22:3–4). Once they arrive at the appointed place, Isaac carries the wood of the sacrifice up the hill (see Genesis 22:6). When he asks his father, "Where is the lamb for the burnt offering?" Abraham responds, "God will provide himself the lamb" (see Genesis 22:7–8).

Abraham binds Isaac and lays him upon the altar. Just as Abraham is about to plunge the knife into his beloved son, the Lord commands Abraham to spare Isaac. Abraham spots a ram, and he offers it to the Lord instead of his son. For the third and final time, God renews his covenant with Abraham, and he swears to bless all of the nations through the seed of Abraham (see Genesis 22:11–18).

This is similar to God's promise in Genesis 3, where he promises to bring deliverance through the "seed" of the woman (Genesis 3:15). Now God promises to save the world through the "seed" of Abraham. Ultimately the woman did not bring salvation to the world: It was her "seed"—the Christ—who became man and was born of a woman. Likewise, salvation will not come through Abraham but through his seed, who is also Christ (see Matthew 1:1).

All of humanity is cursed through the disobedience of Adam. However, all of humanity is blessed through Abraham's obedience. Abraham obeys God by offering his only beloved son. In Abraham the curse of the Fall is partially reversed; through Abraham's "seed," Christ, the curse will be fully reversed.

Three Oaths. In Genesis 15 God promises that Abram's descendants will be delivered from bondage in a foreign nation and will be given the Promised Land (see Genesis 15:13–14). In Genesis 17 God promises that kings will come forth from Abraham and Sarah (see verse 6). And in Genesis 22 God declares that all nations will be blessed through Abraham's descendants (see verse 18).

These three oaths will be fulfilled by the *Exodus* and the *Mosaic covenant,* the *kingdom* and the *Davidic covenant,* and *Jesus Christ* and the *new covenant.*

The Obedience of Abraham and Isaac

Abraham is not the only person who has faith in God; Isaac's obedience is also implied in the biblical narrative. The ancient rabbis called this story the *aqedah* (ah´ kuh duh)—the "binding"—of Isaac (Genesis 22:9). This story is as much about Isaac's self-offering as it is about Abraham's faithfulness. Isaac is a grown youth, strong enough to carry the wood up the moun-

tain (see Genesis 22:6), and thus easily capable of overcoming his elderly father. Therefore Jewish tradition holds that Isaac asked to be bound so that he would not struggle against his father when he was being sacrificed.

The early Church fathers understood this story as a foreshadowing of the sacrifice of Jesus. Like Isaac, Jesus is the only beloved Son of the Father who is sacrificed for the salvation of the world (see Genesis 22:2; John 3:16; Romans 8:32). Like Isaac, Jesus fully submits to his Father's will and carries the wood up the mountain (see Genesis 22:6; John 19:17). Hebrews 11:19 tells us that Abraham was willing to sacrifice his son because he "considered that God was able to raise men even from the dead." Jesus rises from the dead on the third day, just as Abraham received his son back from the sentence of death on the third day (see Genesis 22:4; 1 Corinthians 15:4).

In the Church's liturgy Genesis 22 is read in connection with Jesus' transfiguration. It is during the Transfiguration that the apostles hear God the Father say, "This is my beloved Son" (Mark 9:7). This evokes God's word to Abraham: "Take your son, your only-begotten son Isaac, whom you love, and go to the land of Moriah, and offer him there as a burnt offering upon one of the mountains of which I shall tell you" (see Genesis 22:2). The difference, of course, is that God the Father does not stop the death of his beloved Son but lets Jesus' self-offering fulfill all of the covenants.

Little does Abraham know that his actions foreshadow how God will bring about the blessing of all the nations. In Christ, Abraham's words come true: "God will provide himself the lamb" (Genesis 22:8). Mount Moriah, the place where Abraham offers Isaac, is part of a chain of mountains found outside of Jerusalem. Later in Israel's history the temple of Jerusalem is built on Mount Moriah (see 2 Chronicles 3:1). There the people of Israel offer their sacrifices—in effect reminding God of his covenant promise to Abraham—until the need for these sacrifices ends when Christ comes as the true Lamb of God. Indeed, Calvary—the place where Jesus is crucified—is one of the peaks of Moriah.

A Scriptural Pattern: The Elder Serves the Younger

Abraham's son Isaac has two sons, Esau and Jacob. But just as God chose Abraham's younger son (Isaac) over his elder son (Ishmael), so Jacob is chosen over Esau. This is a subplot that runs throughout the Bible: The younger is chosen over the elder.

God chooses the weaker, younger brother to show that his plans are fulfilled through *his* power, not that of men. Later God preserves Joseph after his older brothers sell him into slav-

ery (see Genesis 37; 39—47). Much later King David is also chosen over his numerous older brothers (see 1 Samuel 16:13).

St. Paul explains: God chooses the younger brother over the older "in order that God's purpose of election might continue, not because of works but because of his call.... So it depends not upon man's will or exertion, but upon God's mercy" (Romans 9:11, 16).

Into Egypt

Just as Abram is renamed Abraham, so Isaac's son Jacob is later renamed Israel. Israel has twelve sons, and they become the fathers of the twelve tribes of the nation of Israel.

The Book of Genesis ends with the familiar story of Joseph. Jacob (or Israel) gives his son Joseph a special coat, and out of jealousy his brothers sell him into slavery. As a slave in Egypt, Joseph receives from the Lord the ability to interpret dreams. Joseph's use of this gift saves the Egyptians and many others from famine. As a result Joseph becomes prime minister of Egypt (see Genesis 41:39-40).

Joseph is reunited with his brothers when they come to Egypt during the famine to buy food. Instead of returning to the land God has given Abraham, Joseph's family remain in Egypt, where they live on the choicest land under his protection. Centuries later a new Pharaoh arises who sees the Hebrews as a threat.

The sons of Israel become enslaved, as God told Abraham they would. They cry to God for help, and he raises up a deliverer, fulfilling his promises to Joseph—"God will be with you, and will bring you again to the land of your fathers" (Genesis 48:21)—and to Abraham that his descendants would be delivered from slavery (see Genesis 15:13-14).

Lesson 5
Moses and the Israelites

God's Firstborn Son

Genesis reveals that salvation history is the story of God's family. God creates Adam as his first-born son of creation. Though Adam sins, God the Father does not give up on humanity. God promises to restore humanity through Abraham (see Genesis 22:18).

The families in Genesis become nations. God calls Abraham's descendants—the nation of Israel—to be his "firstborn son" among the nations. Tragically, like Adam, Israel fails to realize its calling to be a faithful firstborn son. All, however, is not lost. God stoops down to Israel's level as a good father, hoping to raise the nation from its sin to a restored relationship with him.

In Genesis God warns Abraham that his descendants will end up in slavery. He promises, however, to deliver them from bondage and return them to the Promised Land (see Genesis 15:13-16, 18). Exodus tells us how God fulfills his covenant promises.

Although Israel is in servitude in Egypt, God wants to do more than just give the nation *political liberation*. The Scriptures show us that the Israelites were actually in the worst kind of bondage: They were in *spiritual* bondage. The Book of Ezekiel tells us that the Israelites begin worshiping the gods of Egypt before the Exodus (see Ezekiel 20:6-9). Thus the goal of the Exodus is more than political independence: It is to call Israel out of Egypt to worship the Lord. God tells Moses to say on his behalf to Pharaoh, "Let my people go, that they may serve me in the wilderness" (Exodus 7:16). God wants to deliver Israel from serving and worshipping the gods of Egypt so that they can serve and worship him, the *true* God.

The Call of Moses

Fearing the growing Hebrew population, Pharaoh orders the slaughter of all the male Hebrew children (see Exodus 1:8, 15-22). One mother is able to save her child from death by placing him in a basket in the reeds at the edge of the Nile River. One of Pharaoh's daughters finds the child in the water, and she takes him into her home and raises him as her own son. She names the child Moses, which means "taken from water" (Exodus 2:1-10).

Forty years later Moses sees an Egyptian taskmaster beating one of his fellow Hebrews. Moses intervenes and kills the taskmaster. Then he has to flee into the desert, a wanted man. He eventually settles down with a Midianite family and becomes a shepherd (see Exodus 2:11-25).

Forty years later, while he is tending his flock one day, Moses spots a burning bush whose flames seem inextinguishable. When he approaches the bush, God calls to him. The Lord identifies himself as the God of Abraham, Isaac, and Jacob. He tells Moses that he has heard the cry of his enslaved people, and he promises to deliver them and bring them to the Promised Land (see Exodus 3:6–8).

God relates his plan to Moses: Moses is to ask Pharaoh to let Israel go on a three-day journey into the wilderness to sacrifice to the Lord. God tells Moses that Pharaoh will harden his heart and refuse Moses' request. Because of this, God will bring judgment on the Egyptians. He will lead the Israelites out of bondage and bring them into the Promised Land (see Exodus 3:18–20).

God calls Israel to be his "firstborn son" among the nations. When Pharaoh refuses to release God's firstborn son, the Lord will slay Pharaoh's firstborn son (see Exodus 4:22–23).

Deliverance From Egypt

Moses explains to Pharaoh why the Israelites must be allowed to go out to the desert to offer their sacrifices to the Lord: Their sacrifices would be "abominable" to the Egyptians (see Exodus 8:25–27), because Israel is to sacrifice to God the very animals that the Egyptians worship as gods. God wants Israel to renounce the gods of Egypt and to worship him as the one true God.

When Pharaoh refuses to let the people go, God responds by sending ten famous plagues to Egypt. These plagues symbolize judgment on the gods of Egypt. Even after nine plagues, however, Pharaoh still refuses to release God's firstborn son, Israel. Because of this insubordination, God threatens the firstborn sons of the Egyptians. The Lord tells Moses that he will send his angel of death to slay the firstborn sons in Egypt and the firstborn male offspring of all livestock (see Exodus 11:4–9). God also gives Israel a way to save their firstborn sons: the Passover (see Exodus 12:1–27).

The Israelites are instructed to *sacrifice* unblemished lambs, *spread* the blood over their doorposts, and *eat* the lambs as part of a sacred meal (see Exodus 12:5–11). All of the Israelites who obey are "passed over," and their firstborn sons are spared (see Exodus 12:13).

The death of his firstborn son is the event that finally breaks Pharaoh (see Exodus 12:30–32), and he drives the people of Israel out of the land. God appears before Israel as a pillar of cloud by day and a pillar of fire by night. He leads his people out of Egypt and through the Red Sea (see Exodus 13:21; see 14—15).

Even when the Israelites doubt God and complain against him, the Lord cares for his people. The people grow weary of the difficult journey, and they begin to grumble against Moses and the Lord. They complain that they are *hungry*, and the Lord sends miraculous bread from heaven to feed them (see Exodus 16). Then they protest that there is no *water*, so the Lord gives them miraculous water from a rock (see Exodus 17).

St. Paul explains that this foreshadows the new covenant: Just as the Holy Spirit led Israel through the Red Sea under Moses, so we are baptized into Christ and the Spirit in the baptismal waters. Furthermore, Moses gave the people heavenly bread and supernatural drink; Jesus gives us the Eucharist (see 1 Corinthians 10:1–4).

When the Israelites enter the desert, their major issue is trust: Will the people trust God to provide for their needs? Will they be content with God's provision (see Genesis 22:8, 14)? Or will they murmur against God, assuming he will not provide?

The First Covenant With Israel

The Lord brings his people to Mount Sinai. There he declares they are a "kingdom of priests and a holy nation" (see Exodus 19:6). He gives Israel the Ten Commandments (see Exodus 20:1–17; 32:16). In addition he gives them civil laws, telling them how to deal with certain criminal actions (see Exodus 21—23).

Moses builds an altar with twelve pillars, symbolizing that all twelve tribes will enter into the covenant. Then Israel offers sacrifice to God. Moses calls the blood of the sacrificed animals "the blood of the covenant which the LORD has made with you" (Exodus 24:8). The covenant is ratified with a meal when Moses and the elders eat in the presence of God (see Exodus 24:9–11).

God's covenant directions climax when Moses ascends the mountain of the Lord and fasts there for forty days and forty nights (see Exodus 24:15–18). There he receives a vision of a heavenly pattern for the tent of worship, the mobile temple (see Exodus 25:9). Ancient Israelites understood this to mean that Moses saw the heavenly temple, of which the earthly tent and temple were a copy. The Book of Hebrews tells us that those who serve in the earthly temple "serve a copy and shadow of the heavenly sanctuary" (Hebrews 8:5).

The prophets also have visions of the heavenly temple. Isaiah is caught up to the heavenly throne room, where he sees the cherubim before the Lord (see Isaiah 6). It is the apostle John, however, who provides the fullest description of the heavenly Jerusalem in the Apocalypse (see Revelation 21—22).

God's Second Covenant With Israel

Tragically, while Moses is up on the mountain, Israel reverts to the idolatrous practices of the Egyptians. The people construct an image of the Egyptian god Apis, a bull god (see Exodus 32:1–6). Though God brought Israel out of Egypt, taking Egypt out of Israel proves more difficult.

In worshipping the golden calf, Israel succumbs to three major temptations: money, sex, and power. First, the people surrender to the idol of *wealth* by worshipping the *golden* calf. Second, the worship of Apis also involves *sexual immorality* (see Exodus 32:6, 25). Finally, the bull-god represents *virility*, *power*, and *strength*.

When Israel breaks the covenant, the nation deserves the covenant curse of death. Speaking to Moses, God does not refer to Israel as "*my* people" but as "*your* people, whom *you* brought up out of the land of Egypt" (Exodus 32:7; see 3:10; 5:1; 6:7). God tells Moses, "Let me alone, that my wrath may burn hot against them and I may consume them" (Exodus 32:10).

Moses, however, reminds God of his oath to Abraham. If God destroys the Israelites, he will be killing Abraham's chosen descendants. That would break his promise to bless all the nations through them (see Exodus 32:13).

God has not forgotten his oath. He wants Moses to realize why he swore it to Abraham: He knew that Israel would need it. God programmed the covenant with merciful provisions that he knew the people would need.

Moses comes down from the mountain and, upon seeing the idolatry of Israel, smashes the tablets of the Ten Commandments (see Exodus 32:15–19). This symbolizes what Israel has done: The people have broken their covenant with the Lord. Then Moses shouts, "Who is on the Lord's side?"

The Levites respond, and Moses instructs them to kill the idolaters. Three thousand Israelites die because of their idolatry that day (see Exodus 32:26–28). Moses then tells the Levites, "Today you have ordained yourselves for the service of the LORD, each one at the cost of his son and of his brother, that he may bestow a blessing upon you this day" (Exodus 32:29).

Now the covenant law changes. Israel has revealed its spiritual bondage to the gods of Egypt. To help purify the people of their idolatrous tendencies, God gives Moses an elaborate code of ritual purity laws, recounted in the Book of Leviticus. These laws are designed, in part, to

quarantine Israel from the gentiles and their practices. These purity laws imply that Israel is not yet holy enough to go out and evangelize the nations. The people must first learn humility.

Moreover, God gives exhaustive instructions for continual animal sacrifice. Since the Israelites worshipped a golden calf, they must regularly sacrifice calves, sheep, and goats, renouncing the gods of Egypt.

Prior to their sin Israel was called a "kingdom of priests" (Exodus 19:6). Now the Levites alone shall serve as priests. Thus the Book of Leviticus explains to the Levites the purity laws of the priests (see Leviticus 1—16) and the laws they are to teach the people to make them holy (see Leviticus 17—26).

Rebellions and Rules

The Israelites continue to rebel. The Book of Numbers presents a pattern throughout its pages: Israel sins, and God gives Israel more laws. The laws are means to teach Israel to acknowledge her weakness and turn to the Lord (see Galatians 3:19).

When the Israelites finally arrive at the border of the land promised to them, they refuse to enter into it. They fear those who inhabit the land, even though the Lord has promised them the land and victory over those who dwell in it (see Numbers 13:30—14:10).

By rejecting the Lord, the Israelites prove that they are beyond rehabilitation. The Lord promises that the current generation—except for Joshua and Caleb—will never enter the land. They will wander the desert until they die. The Lord will bring the next generation into the land (see Numbers 14:20‒35).

Sadly, however, forty years later the next generation proves to be no less wicked. They fall into the sin of idolatry, just as their fathers did before them, to Ba'al at Peor (see Numbers 25).

Deuteronomy means "second law"; due to their sinfulness God gives Israel a "lower law." Deuteronomy, therefore, is not promulgated in the words of God but in the words of Moses. The book makes concessions, such as permitting divorce and genocidal warfare, that are absent in previous covenant legislations. According to Jesus, Moses gives these lower laws to Israel due to the hardness of their heart (see Ezekiel 20:25; Matthew 19:8).

The fathers of the Church recognized this "divine condescension" as an example of how our heavenly Father stoops down to the level of his children. The Deuteronomic Law was meant to

teach Israel how to "grow up" in holiness. When Christ comes, however, these Deuteronomic law codes are no longer necessary (see Galatians 3:25).

The Book of Deuteronomy also recounts the instructions that Moses gives Israel for reconquering the land promised to Abraham, Isaac, and Jacob. The conditions of the Deuteronomic covenant will be fulfilled when the Lord gives Israel "rest from all your enemies round about" (Deuteronomy 12:10). At that time the Lord will show Israel where they are to build the temple (see Deuteronomy 12:11). In other words, the goal of Deuteronomy, just like the Book of Exodus, concerns liturgy and worship, not just political independence. God wants Israel to worship him, and once the instructions of Deuteronomy are fulfilled, the nation will worship in a temple.

Jesus as the New Moses

The person and work of Jesus is foreshadowed in Moses and the events of Israel's Passover and Exodus. Like Moses, Jesus is born during the reign of a ruthless king who kills other Hebrew male children. Like Israel, Jesus sojourns in Egypt and is called back to his birthplace after a period of exile. He passes through waters—his baptism in the Jordan—and goes out into the wilderness, where he is tested by a forty-day fast.

Jesus' first miracle is turning water into wine, and he later turns wine into blood, recalling the first plague of Exodus. He teaches from a mountain, just as Moses' teaching issued from his visitation on a mountain. Jesus' appearance on a mountain before three companions radiates God's glory, just as Moses' face shone on his descent from the mountain after speaking with God (see Exodus 34:29–35). Jesus gives heavenly bread and spiritual drink to God's people (the Eucharist), as foreshadowed by the manna in the desert. He appoints a set of twelve leaders (the apostles) and then an additional set of seventy disciples, just as Moses appointed judges to help him govern Israel in the desert (see Matthew 10:1; Numbers 11:16–17). Jesus is the true Passover Lamb, and he leads us out of spiritual bondage in the New Exodus.

Thus God uses the historical events in the Old Testament to prefigure the salvation Christ brings in the New. Through Israel's Passover God delivers the nation from bondage and slavery and leads them to the Promised Land. In the new Passover Christ delivers us from the bondage of sin and leads us to the heavenly Jerusalem, the true Promised Land.

Furthermore, Israel's Passover prefigures the paschal mystery of the new covenant. In Israel's Passover a lamb is sacrificed, its blood shed, and its body eaten as part of a family meal. In the true Passover Christ is offered as the sacrificial Lamb of God. His blood is shed for the salva-

tion of the world. Just as the Israelites had to eat the lamb, so the Church feeds upon the Body and Blood of Christ in the Eucharist. The Lamb has been sacrificed; now we must partake of the meal (see 1 Corinthians 5:7–8). In fact, Christ's words at the Last Supper evoke the covenant ratification ceremony at Sinai (see Matthew 26:27; Exodus 24:1–8).

Lesson 6

The Covenant With David

Into the Promised Land

After Moses dies Joshua finally brings the Israelites into the land that was promised to Abraham, Isaac, and Jacob/Israel (see Joshua 3—4). Joshua leads Israel in a series of battles to take back the land from the wicked people who took it while the Israelites were slaves in Egypt (see Joshua 6; 8—12). After they reclaim their land, Joshua allots portions to each tribe (see Joshua 13—21).

Israel fights for generations against the Canaanites under certain men and women—called judges—whom God raises up to lead the people in a series of victories. Throughout the time of the judges, there is a three-D cycle: (1) *Disobedience*: One or more tribes become complacent about covenant faithfulness; (2) *Defeat*: God allows an enemy to humble the Israelites through defeat and servitude; (3) *Deliverance*: The Israelites cry out to God for help, and he sends a judge to deliver them and govern them in peace for a time. This cycle repeats many times.

Saul, the First King

Samuel—the last of the judges, a priest, and a prophet—wants his sons to take his place, but the elders of Israel say it's time for a change. They want Samuel to appoint a king so they can be governed as other nations are (see 1 Samuel 8:1-5). Samuel anoints Saul as the first king of Israel (see 1 Samuel 10:1). God exalts the humble when he chooses Saul from the smallest tribe, the tribe of Benjamin—the tribe of the youngest brother of the twelve sons of Israel (see 1 Samuel 9:21).

Saul, however, falls into error and disobeys God. For his disobedience he first loses his dynasty and then his throne.

David's Rise to Power

Without telling Saul, Samuel goes to the house of Jesse in Bethlehem, where he anoints David (the youngest of eight sons) as the second king of Israel (see 1 Samuel 16:11-13). David is a man after God's own heart (see 1 Samuel 13:14). For the honor of God's name, he defeats the Philistine champion Goliath with a slingshot (see 1 Samuel 17). He subsequently becomes a part of Saul's household, soothing Saul during his fits by playing music on his lyre. Saul doesn't know that this is the future king—filled with God's Spirit—who is calming him.

When Saul realizes, however, that David is God's anointed one, he tries to hunt David down to kill him. David, out of respect for Saul's office, does not kill Saul, even when he has an opportunity to do so. Later on, when King Saul and his sons perish (see 1 Samuel 31), David laments over Saul and Jonathan (see 2 Samuel 1). He also offers a permanent place in his home and at his table for Saul's only living grandson, Mephibosheth (see 2 Samuel 9).

David conquers the last stronghold of the Canaanites, the famous city of Jerusalem (see 2 Samuel 4:6–10). Here God desires to dwell in the midst of his people, now that they have defeated their enemies (see Deuteronomy 12:10–11). David realizes that the Deuteronomic covenant has been fulfilled. He expresses his desire to build a temple (see 2 Samuel 7:1–2; Psalm 132), but God has other plans.

David as Liturgical Leader

At Mount Sinai God called Israel to be a "kingdom of priests" (Exodus 19:6), but they failed to achieve this calling. Now God establishes the son of David on Jerusalem's Mount Zion as a priest-king through whom Israel's calling is restored.

David is a king, but he also aspires to *priestly* service. He wears a Levitical garment; he leads the procession of the ark of the covenant from the house of Obededom into the tabernacle in Jerusalem; he offers sacrifices; he blesses the people in the name of the Lord; and he serves the people bread, meat, and wine (see 2 Samuel 6:14–19). He also writes numerous songs for use in Israel's worship, many of which are ascribed to him in the Book of Psalms.

God makes David a king and a priest. Not only does David conquer the land and rule as king, but he also receives the blueprint for the temple and its worship (see 1 Chronicles 28:19). He organizes the liturgical celebration, including the duties of the Levites, ministers, and choirs in the tabernacle (see 1 Chronicles 15:16–24). And he also commands the Levites to offer thank offerings (*todah*) perpetually before the ark (the sign of God's presence in the tabernacle).

Primary Features of the Davidic Covenant

The Davidic covenant is the final covenant between God and Israel. It is the "climax" of the Old Testament.

1. The Son of David is the Son of God. God swears that David's son will be God's son (see 2 Samuel 7:14; Psalm 2:7). On the day of his enthronement, the Davidic king is anointed by a Levite. Once he is anointed, he is God's son. The Davidic king is thus called God's "first-born" (Psalm 89:27). In the Davidic king Israel's original calling finds partial fulfillment.

2. The Davidic king is a "Messiah." In Hebrew the word for "anointed one," *mashiach* [mah she´ ah], means "messiah." The royal anointing is associated with the reception of God's Spirit (see 1 Samuel 16:13). David (see Psalm 89:19–21), Solomon (see 1 Kings 1:32–40), and other Davidic kings (see 2 Kings 11:12; 23:30; 2 Chronicles 23:11) are all anointed.

Jesus is the true anointed one of God. The Greek word for "anointed one" is *Christos.* Jesus is the "son of David" according to the genealogy of Joseph (Matthew 1:1). Jesus is baptized by John the Baptist (a Levite), whose father is a priest (see Luke 1:5; John 1:32). Following Jesus' baptism, the Holy Spirit descends on him, and God declares Jesus to be his beloved Son (see Mark 1:9–11). Immediately following his baptism, Jesus announces the coming of the kingdom of God.

3. The Davidic kingdom is international. God's covenant with Israel under Moses was national in scope; his covenant with David is international in scope. David's royal cabinet includes non-Israelites (see 1 Chronicles 11:11–12). Solomon establishes covenant treaties with other nations, like Tyre (see 1 Kings 5:1–12). Psalm 72 describes Solomon's reign in universal terms (verses 8 and 11). God's covenant extends through the kingdom to all nations (see Psalm 2:8).

Jesus instructs the apostles to make disciples of "all nations" (Matthew 28:19). He commissions them to spread the gospel "to the end of the earth" (Acts 1:8; see 13:47).

4. The Davidic kingdom is located in Jerusalem. Jerusalem is the political capital for the Davidic kingdom, but Mount Zion, in Jerusalem, is to be the spiritual center of Israel, the place where nations will gather before God's presence. Psalm 87:5 states that peoples of all nations will be united to the Lord on Mount Zion.

On Mount Zion, in the Upper Room, Jesus establishes his reign when he institutes the Eucharist. In the same Upper Room his disciples receive the Holy Spirit on Pentecost. The author of the Letter to the Hebrews refers to the heavenly Jerusalem as Mount Zion, the city of the living God, our place of worship (see Hebrews 12:22–24).

5. The temple of Solomon is a place of worship. The temple is the place God chooses for his name to dwell (see 1 Kings 8:27–29). This fulfills Moses' prophecy in Deuteronomy 12:10–12. The temple is a place of prayer and worship for Israel and all of the nations.

Jesus refers to his body as the temple when he predicts that the temple will be destroyed and three days later will be rebuilt (see John 2:19–21). Jesus reigns now in the heavenly temple (see Hebrews 8:5).

6. God gives the king wisdom to build, to govern, and to teach. God asks Solomon what he wants; Solomon asks for wisdom so that he will be able to govern a vast empire justly (see 1

Kings 3:5–12). This pleases God so much that he gives Solomon not only wisdom but also wealth and a long life (see 1 Kings 3:13–14, 28; 4:29). God gives Solomon wisdom to build and dedicate the temple (see 1 Kings 6; 8) and to instruct all nations in God's ways when they seek his wisdom (see 1 Kings 4:34; 10:1–10). Solomon sends God's wisdom throughout the world. Wisdom literature—such as Proverbs, Ecclesiastes, Song of Solomon, and Wisdom of Solomon—is attributed to him.

Jesus is the true Son of David through whom wisdom comes to the world (see 1 Corinthians 1:30). He instructs the nations in the ways of the Father. Through him God's wisdom (the Holy Spirit) is given (see John 12:7–15).

7. *The kingdom is an everlasting kingdom.* David's kingdom is everlasting (see 2 Samuel 7:13; Psalm 89:36–37). The Davidic dynasty is the longest lasting dynasty in recorded history: From 1000 to 586 BC one of David's sons ruled in Jerusalem. No other kingdom has had an unbroken line of dynastic succession comparable to the Davidic dynasty. But a four-hundred-year dynasty is not "everlasting." In 586 BC it seems as though God's promise to David fails. The Davidic king is caught, and his sons are killed before him (see 2 Kings 25:7). But the prophets remind Israel of God's promise: The kingdom will be restored, and a son of David will reign.

In Jesus God's covenant oath is fulfilled. As the Son of David who reigns in heaven, Jesus transfers the kingdom to the heavenly Jerusalem. His kingdom is truly an everlasting kingdom!

Secondary Features of the Davidic Covenant

1. *The queen mother.* Like other kings before and after him, Solomon has more than one wife but only one mother, Bathsheba. Solomon's mother is given a crown and reigns as queen (see 1 Kings 2:19). This exalted position continues throughout the Davidic line and is referred to as the *gebirah* [gib´ e rah]. Since Jesus is the King of Kings, his mother, Mary, is the chosen mother. She serves the kingdom of heaven in an exalted position.

2. *The prime minister.* The prime minister is given *keys* that denote his *authority* and the *succession* involved in this position (see Isaiah 22:15–22). Jesus establishes Peter as his prime minister in Matthew 16:19. Though Peter denies him three times (see Matthew 26:69–75), Jesus commissions Peter to lead the disciples when he appears to them on the beach (see John 21:15–19).

3. *The Todah.* The *Todah* (or "thank offering") becomes the primary liturgy celebrated in the temple (see Leviticus 7:11–15; 1 Chronicles 16). David wrote many *todah* or "thank offering" psalms, which follow a similar pattern of three stages. Psalm 50 illustrates these.

Through the *todah* Israel learned to offer afflictions to God in thanksgiving. The psalms explain that this act of thanksgiving is what the Lord truly wants (see Psalm 69:30–31).

The Greek word for thanksgiving is *eucharistia* [you car ist ee´ uh], from which we get the word *Eucharist.* Jesus offers himself through the Church's eucharistic offering. In this offering we eat consecrated bread and proclaim Christ's death and resurrection over the cup. We also offer ourselves.

The Kingdom Established

One way in which David does not resemble Jesus is in his sin (see 2 Samuel 11). David is not where he is supposed to be: He remains at home instead of leading the troops in battle. He lingers at his window, watching Bathsheba bathe on her roof. He longs for her, though she is the wife of Uriah, a Hittite warrior and one of David's most trusted soldiers.

David invites Bathsheba into his bedchamber, and he commits adultery with her. When she conceives, David tries to cover up his sin. When the cover-up fails, David sets Uriah up to be killed in battle.

The prophet Nathan confronts David and pronounces God's judgment: The sword will never depart out of David's house, and his child will die. David repents deeply, praying Psalm 51, the great psalm of contrition. Then he marries Bathsheba.

When Bathsheba delivers their son, he is very ill, and he dies shortly afterward. David and Bathsheba conceive another son, Solomon, who becomes David's heir to the throne.

Shortly after Solomon's coronation, the three promises made to Abraham in Genesis 12:1–3 are fulfilled: *land and nationhood* (see 1 Kings 4:21); *a great name through a royal dynasty* (see 2 Samuel 7:9; 1 Kings 4:20–21; Genesis 22:17–18); and *worldwide blessing* through God's temple and wisdom (see Psalm 72:17). The movement from Moses and the nation of Israel to David's kingdom—from Sinai to Zion—is complete.

The Fall of the Kingdom and the Promise of Restoration

In anticipation of future kings of Israel, Moses gives three warnings in Deuteronomy 17:16–17: Do not multiply *weapons, wealth,* or *wives.* King Solomon, at first, leads the people in wisdom. Tragically, however, he fails to heed all three warnings: He multiplies *weapons* (horses and chariots used for battle) (see 2 Chronicles 9:25, 28) and *wealth* (see 1 Kings 10:14, 27). His political alliances through marriage result in seven hundred *wives* and three hundred concu-

bines. They in turn draw Solomon's heart away from the Lord (see 1 Kings 11:1–5).

Due to Solomon's sin, God allows the kingdom to be divided after his death. The ten northern tribes rebel against the Davidic king and form the northern kingdom of Israel. The two southern tribes (Judah and Benjamin) form the southern kingdom of Judah, and a Davidic king continues to rule them (see 1 Kings 11:9–40).

In 722 BC the Assyrians conquer the northern kingdom of Israel and permanently scatter the people among the nations. In 586 BC the Babylonians capture the southern kingdom of Judah after they destroy Jerusalem and the temple. After seventy years in exile, the "Judahites" (or "Judeans" or "Jews") return to their land and slowly rebuild the temple under Zarubbabel and then Ezra and Nehemiah. However, they still struggle against their enemies.

In the Mosaic covenant, Israel has a twofold administration. God establishes the Levites to uphold the Law and to coadminister the civic codes with the elders in Israel. God also calls judges—men and women—to rescue the Israelites and rule them by the Spirit.

Something similar happens in the Davidic covenant. Although the Davidic king is the political leader of the people, responsible for the Law, God sends his Spirit upon the prophets. They foretell God's restoration of the Davidic kingdom through a messiah. Isaiah 53:4–6 states that the Messiah will not be triumphant by winning a great military battle. On the contrary, he will suffer greatly, but through his sufferings he will atone for sins. The Messiah will offer himself as a sacrifice to God. Jeremiah 31:31–34 explains that through the Messiah, God will establish a "new covenant" to restore his family. Through the new covenant, God's plan to make us his covenant family will be fulfilled (see Jeremiah 32:36–41).

The future Son of David will defeat evil once and for all. He will restore the kingdom as God's worldwide covenant family.

Lesson 7
Jesus: Fulfillment of the Promises

Salvation history reveals how God works through the covenants of the Old Testament to make us his family. In the person and work of Jesus Christ in the new covenant, God fulfills his promises to Adam, Abraham, Moses, and David.

New Adam in the Garden

While the first Adam was disobedient in the garden, Jesus (the New Adam) goes into a garden and prays, "Your will be done" (Matthew 26:42). His obedience undoes what Adam's disobedience has done.

Adam triggered the curse of the covenant: He was ashamed and naked (see Genesis 3:10); his work became toilsome and not always fruitful (see Genesis 3:18); his labor was difficult and sweat-producing (see Genesis 3:18); and his physical death was inevitable (see Genesis 3:19). Jesus bears the covenant curses redemptively: His sweat is like drops of blood (see Luke 22:44); he wears a crown of thorns (see Matthew 27:29); he is stripped naked (see Matthew 27:31); and he is put to death.

The Son of Abraham

On the third day the Father receives his only beloved Son back from the dead. Through Jesus' resurrection God fulfills the oath he swore to Abraham in Genesis 22:18 to bless all nations through Abraham's seed.

Little did Abraham realize that God was using him and his son Isaac to foreshadow the way this covenant oath would be fulfilled. When Abraham offered his only beloved son on Mount Moriah, he told Isaac, "God will provide himself the lamb" (Genesis 22:8). Abraham believed that Isaac was the son of promise and that God could resurrect him if need be (Hebrews 11:19).

The first verse in the New Testament identifies Jesus as "the son of Abraham." Jesus is the only beloved Son of the Father (see John 3:16). He offers himself as a sacrifice to God on Calvary (one of the peaks of Moriah). Like Isaac, he carries the wood of the sacrifice up the mountain, and there God provides himself as the Lamb. On the third day the Father raises his Son from the dead—just as Abraham received his son back on the third day (see Genesis 22:4). In short, through his death and resurrection, Jesus fulfills God's promise to Abraham to bless all the nations (see Galatians 3:13–14).

The New Moses

Jesus' birth parallels Moses' birth. Both Jesus and Moses are born during the reign of a ruthless king; both tyrants kill other Hebrew male children ("the slaughter of the innocents"). Both Jesus and Moses find safety in Egypt. Finally, after the tyrants' deaths, both come out of Egypt, pass through waters, and are led into the desert.

Ministry. Jesus fasts for forty days and forty nights, as did Moses. Jesus is tempted by Satan in the desert, just as Israel was tested in the wilderness. To rebuke the devil, Jesus cites the very passages from Deuteronomy 6—8 where Moses explained to Israel why they failed the test they faced in the wilderness (see Matthew 4:1-10; Luke 4:1-13).

After his forty-day fast, Jesus begins his public ministry by declaring the new covenant law on a mountain (Matthew 5—7), the Sermon on the Mount. After his forty days' fast, Moses also gave Israel the Law of God from a mountain—Mount Sinai. Jesus' mission is to fulfill God's Word —*not* to abolish the Law and the prophets (see Matthew 5:17). Thus he does not relax the Law of Moses; he *internalizes* it and *intensifies* it. For example, while Moses commanded Israel not to commit adultery, Jesus states that anyone who even looks lustfully at a woman commits adultery with her in his heart (see Matthew 5:31-32).

What Moses gave is great; what Jesus gives is greater (see John 1:17). Jesus challenges the Israelites to allow the Scriptures (and Moses' writings in particular) to bear witness to him (see John 5:39, 46-47).

Signs and Miracles. Throughout his life and ministry, Jesus works signs and miracles. The Gospel of John records Jesus' first "sign" at the wedding feast at Cana (see John 2:1-11). There Jesus turns water in the stone jars into wine. Moses' first sign was turning water into blood, including water in "vessels of stone" (Exodus 7:19).

Another sign Jesus performs is the miraculous feeding of the crowds (see John 6:5-14). Jesus multiplies the loaves of bread and the fish so that twelve baskets are left over (symbolizing the twelve tribes of Israel). Moses fed Israel with miraculous bread from heaven (see Exodus 16:2-30). Unlike Moses, however, Jesus himself is the true Bread from heaven (see John 6:32, 35).

Friends and Coworkers. Though Jesus and Moses both have the Law and miraculous power, they choose coworkers to assist them in caring for God's people. Jesus appoints twelve apostles (see Luke 6:13-16), and later he appoints seventy disciples (see Luke 10:1). Moses also

sends out twelve tribal princes (see Numbers 13) and appoints seventy elders to assist him (Numbers 11). Jesus' inner circle includes Peter, James, and John; Moses' inner circle includes Aaron, Nadab, and Abihu (see Exodus 24:1; 28:1).

Transfigured on a Mountain. The Transfiguration underlines Jesus' role as the new Moses. Jesus goes up a mountain with three companions (see Luke 9:28), as did Moses (see Exodus 24:1, 15). Jesus' appearance is transfigured in the midst of God's presence in the glory-cloud (see Luke 9:29), as was Moses' (see Exodus 34:29–35). Jesus speaks to Moses (the giver of the Law) and Elijah (the greatest prophet) about his "departure" (that is, his "exodus"— Luke 9:30–31). The evangelists see Jesus as a New Moses who leads a new exodus and gives a new law.

The Passover Celebrated and Fulfilled

The Gospels show us how Jesus celebrates the Passover and transforms it into the Eucharist (see Matthew 26:26–29). Jesus sends Peter and John to make preparations for the Passover (see Luke 22:7–13). He institutes the Eucharist as a memorial (see Luke 22:19, "in remembrance"), just as the Passover was a "memorial" (see Exodus 12:14). Jesus blesses the cup, calling it the "blood of the covenant" (Matthew 26:28), reminiscent of Moses sealing the covenant with Israel with the blood of the sacrifice, which he called "the blood of the covenant" (Exodus 24:8).

The Gospel of John describes how Jesus fulfills the Passover through his passion and death (see John 19). The soldiers take Jesus to be crucified at the sixth hour—the hour the high priest begins to slaughter Passover lambs (see John 19:14). John explains that the soldiers do not break Jesus' legs—fulfilling the prescription that the Passover lamb have no broken bones or blemishes (see John 19:32–36; Exodus 12:46). Further, John notes that Jesus is wearing a seamless garment like that worn by the high priest (see John 19:23; Exodus 28:32). Finally, the soldiers raise a sponge of vinegar to Jesus' mouth on a hyssop branch, which is the kind of branch used to sprinkle the blood of the Passover lamb (see John 19:29; Exodus 12:21–23).

All of this demonstrates that the Eucharist—which is the new Passover—and Calvary are inseparable. They are one and the same sacrifice.

What Jesus begins in the Upper Room he concludes on the cross. The bread becomes Jesus' body, which is "given for you" (Luke 22:19). The wine is Jesus' blood, which is "poured out for you" (Luke 22:20). Here Jesus evokes the image of the Levitical priests, who were instructed by Moses to "pour out" the blood of the sacrifice (Exodus 29:12; Leviticus 4:7). Through the Eucharist Jesus offers himself to the Father (see Isaiah 55:3–12).

The work of salvation is not complete with Jesus' death for our sins. We are saved by the cross *and* the Resurrection (Romans 4:24–25). This Resurrection is more than resuscitation from the dead or the vindication of an innocent man. In his resurrection Jesus' humanity is divinized—glorified (see CCC, 651–655); and by uniting ourselves to him, we share in his glorified humanity. In a very real sense, the Resurrection is the climax of God's covenant plan (see 1 Corinthians 15:20–22, 42–45).

The Son of David

Matthew's Gospel begins with Jesus' genealogy: He is the "son of David" (Matthew 1:1). Jesus' birthplace is the same as David's, Bethlehem (see 1 Samuel 16:1; Matthew 2:1).

Jesus is the "anointed one," the true Davidic king. In the last lesson we saw how the Davidic king was always anointed by a Levite (see 1 Kings 1:34; 2 Kings 11:12; 23:30; 2 Chronicles 23:11). Matthew 3 records that Jesus was baptized by John the Baptist, a Levite, and "after the baptism which John preached…God anointed Jesus of Nazareth with the Holy Spirit and with power" (Acts 10:37–38).

Once anointed, the king was declared the adopted son of God (see Psalm 2:7). Already the eternal Son of God, Jesus becomes the Son of David by God's grace and mercy. John the Baptist hears the Father's declaration, "This is my beloved Son" (Matthew 3:17).

Jesus begins his public ministry by preaching "the gospel of the kingdom" (Matthew 4:23). This is his primary theme. His Sermon on the Mount begins with eight Beatitudes that begin and end with the promise "Theirs is the kingdom of heaven" (Matthew 5:3, 10).

In Matthew 6 Jesus gives us the Our Father, in which we are to pray, "Thy kingdom come" (Matthew 6:10). He also urges the people to seek the kingdom above all (see Matthew 6:33).

In Matthew 7 Jesus describes the ideal disciple in terms reminiscent of Solomon. He also tells us that his wisdom is greater than that of Solomon (see Matthew 12:42); and like Solomon, he teaches in parables (see Matthew 13).

Matthew records Jesus' ministry to gentiles as well as Israelites: He heals the centurion's son (see Matthew 8:5–13) and a Canaanite woman (see Matthew 15:22–28), and he casts a demon out of a Syrophoenician woman's daughter (see Mark 7:24–30). The crowds that gather to hear him include people from outside Israel, "from about Tyre and Sidon" (Mark 3:8).

Jesus doesn't simply "take" the kingdom away to heaven. The kingdom is present on earth through the ministry of the apostles, especially through Peter (see Matthew 16:18–19). The Greek word for "assembly" (*ekklesia*) translates to "church" in English. Just as Solomon built the temple on the rock, so Jesus builds the Church on Peter, the "rock."

Jesus also gives Peter the "keys" of the kingdom. Keys in the Old Testament symbolized the prime minister's authority in the kingdom: He was given the authority to "shut" and "open," and he was called to be a "father" (see Isaiah 22:20–22). Jesus employs similar language when he gives Peter the keys: He gives authority to Peter to "bind" and "loose" (Matthew 16:19). Peter is also called to be a father, as *pope* means "father." Thus, through the Church's ministry, the kingdom Christ established in heaven is present now on earth.

The Gospel writers understood that on Palm Sunday, Jesus as the Son of David came to the city of David to restore the kingdom of David (see Mark 11:10; Luke 19:38). Instead of riding triumphantly into Jerusalem, however, Jesus arrives humbly on a donkey—just as Solomon did (see Matthew 21:6–7; 1 Kings 1:38). The people shout, "Hosanna to the Son of David!" (Matthew 21:9), but Jesus' triumph as the Davidic king will not come through political or military strength.

The Kingdom Banquet

In Luke's Gospel the Passover meal is intimately connected to the coming of the kingdom. Jesus tells the apostles, "I shall not eat it until it is fulfilled in the kingdom of God" (Luke 22:16), and, "I shall not drink of the fruit of the vine until the kingdom of God comes" (Luke 22:18). He also tells them that they will eat and drink at his table and sit on thrones in the kingdom (see Luke 22:30).

The disciples' dispute about how the kingdom will be administered is placed in the middle of this passage. Jesus challenges them not to lord it over others but rather to follow his example as a king who serves at the table (see Luke 22:27).

Jesus not only institutes the Eucharist but also ordains the priests who will follow his example and offer this sacrifice "in remembrance" of him. *Remembrance* is liturgical language.

As the apostles continue with Jesus through his trials, they receive a call: Jesus appoints (or "covenants") them to imitate him as king, to exercise royal authority, and to extend the kingdom—all of which they will do as they offer the Eucharist. It is significant that the only kingdom "covenanted" in Scripture is the kingdom of David (see Psalm 89:19–37). This is the kingdom that foreshadows Christ's kingdom.

David moved the thank offering (the *todah*) to the center of Israel's liturgical life. *Todah* (when translated into Greek) is *Eucharist,* meaning "thanksgiving." On the cross Jesus prays Psalm 22—a *todah* psalm. He appeals to God to vindicate him, to save him. Though he begins with the first verse, speaking of abandonment, the psalm concludes with praise to God for his deliverance.

The Last Supper is Jesus' *todah* meal. Through the Eucharist we share in the *todah* of our Davidic Priest-King: We proclaim Christ's death and resurrection, and we offer ourselves through Christ's offering. Furthermore, through the Eucharist we enter into the kingdom, the family of God—the Trinity—and thus God's covenant plan is accomplished.

As we offer ourselves to God in the Eucharist, we receive a foretaste of heaven. Wherever the King is, there is the kingdom; and wherever the Eucharist is, there is the King!

The Kingdom Restored

After his resurrection Jesus appears to the apostles, and then he remains with them for forty days. Acts 1:3 tells us that he speaks to them about "the kingdom of God." The apostles are eager for the restoration of the kingdom (see Acts 1:6). Jesus explains that the kingdom will be restored when they receive the Holy Spirit. The apostles will be "witnesses in Jerusalem and… Judea and Samaria, and to the end of the earth" (Acts 1:8). This is a map of the Davidic kingdom under Solomon. (Psalm 72:8 describes Solomon's reign extending "to the ends of the earth.")

Thus, through the ministry of the Church in Acts, the kingdom is restored. The Book of Acts begins with Jesus and then St. Peter proclaiming the kingdom. In his inaugural sermon at Pentecost, Peter uses the Psalms to show how the Resurrection and the Ascension represent the fulfillment of the Davidic covenant (see Acts 2:29–36).

At the center of the Book of Acts is the Jerusalem Council, where the apostles deal with the admission of gentiles into the Church. St. James recognizes that the kingdom of David is restored, for Israelites as well as gentiles, through the Church (see Acts 15:12–21).

Acts ends with St. Paul's preaching of the kingdom in Rome (see Acts 28:31). He addresses the Christians in Rome (Israelites and gentiles) with a declaration of Jesus as the Son of David and the Son of God (see Romans 1:1–4). Through God's kingdom his covenant is extended to all nations.

Through the Resurrection the Davidic King conquers death, fulfilling God's oath to David to establish his kingdom forever (see 2 Samuel 7:13). Through the Ascension Jesus transfers the kingdom to heaven. Hebrews 12:22–23 notes that we "have come to Mount Zion and to…the heavenly Jerusalem." Established in heaven, the kingdom will never be shaken.